THE BOOK CASINO MANAGERS FEAR THE MOST!

Marvin Karlins Ph.D.

GOLLEHON BOOKS™

GRAND RAPIDS, MICHIGAN

Library of Congress Catalog Card Number 98-70697

ISBN 0-914839-45-4
(International Standard Book Number)

GOLLEHON is an exclusive trademark of Gollehon Press, Inc.

GOLLEHON BOOKS are published by: Gollehon Press, Inc.,
6157 28th St. SE, Grand Rapids, MI 49546.

GOLLEHON BOOKS are available in quantity purchases;
contact Special Sales. Gollehon does not accept unsolicited
manuscripts. Brief book proposals are reviewed.

To Edy, my wife; and Amber, my daughter:
Two natural winners on the pass-line of life.

Contents

Section One: The Two Questions You Must Ask Yourself Before You Ever Gamble Again

1. Do You Know How To Win? 1

2. Do You Know Why You Gamble? 5

Section Two: The Two Things You Need to Know About Casinos: How They Use You; How You Can Use Them

3. How Casinos Are Designed To Make You Lose . . . 15

4. How You Can Use Casinos To Help You Win! 56

Section Three: The Three Levels of Gambling Stupidity That Cost You Money: Dumb, Dumber, And Dumbest

5. Domain Of The Dumb 89

6. Domicile Of The Dumber 97

7. Dominion Of The Dumbest 101

Section Four: The Four Psychobiological Keys To Winning In The Casino

8. Overcoming Your Psychological Governors 110

9. Eliminating The "AIR" Of Your Ways 136

10. Using Biorhythms For Betting 143

11. Winning Your Wager Against Excessive Stress . . . 157

**Section Five: The Four Death Sentences In A Casino...
And What You Can Do To Overturn Them**

12. Death Sentence #1: "I Didn't Come All
    The Way Out Here To Break Even." 167

13. Death Sentence #2: "Wait Here A Moment
    While I Make A Bet To Cover Dinner." 172

14. Death Sentence #3: "Take My Bags Upstairs...
    I Want To Check Out The Casino Before I Go
    To My Room." 176

15. Death Sentence #4: "Give Me Back The Money
    I Told You Not To Give Me Back." 181

**Section Six: The Eight Gambling Questions Players
Ask Me The Most**

16. Question #1: "Should I Go On A Junket? 186

17. Question #2: "Can Money Management Help
    Me In The Casino?" 195

18. Question #3: "Should I Gamble In Casinos
    Outside The United States?" 203

19. Question #4: "Is It Possible To Beat The Slots?" . 211

20. Question #5: "Should I Play In Casino
    Tournaments?" 222

21. Question #6: "Do Casinos Cheat?" 232

22. Question #7: "Can I Make A Living At Casino
    Gambling?" 237

23. Question #8: "What Is A 'Compulsive' Gambler?" 241

SECTION ONE

The Two Questions You Must Ask Yourself Before You Ever Gamble Again

1st Gambler: "Why did you play if you knew the game was crooked?"
2nd Gambler: "Because it was the only game in town."

Anonymous

CHAPTER 1

Do You Know
How To Win?

I love those players who know how to lose;
I fear those players who know how to win.
Casino Manager

Do *you* know how to win in a casino?

Think about it. Are you ahead of the game? Do you strike fear in the hearts of casino managers when you saunter into their establishments? When you finish playing do you worry about how to get all that winning cash safely home?

You know what *I* think?

I think not! In fact, when it comes to casino gambling, I strongly suspect you've made your "contribution." Maybe not every session, possibly not every trip, but overall, I'll bet you 2–to–1 that your gaming ledger is hemorrhaging red ink.

Why? Because the way most people gamble, the odds are stacked against them 3–to–1 the moment they enter a casino. First, they're battling the house percentages at the tables; second, they're combating the casino tactics designed to make them lose; and third, they're fighting themselves.

Hey, do you think places like "Lost Wages, Nevada" were built from funds donated by *winning* gamblers?

Which brings us to the critical question of this book: *Can you learn to win in casinos throughout the world?*

Affirmative.

I'll tell you how to do it... and that's why casino managers fear this book. It could cost them their jobs. In fact, **if every casino player would follow all the tactics set forth in this book, every legal casino in the world would go bankrupt within a few short years.**

Whoa! Don't just breeze through that last paragraph. *Think* about it. You are holding in your hands the ammunition you need to destroy the casino. Will it happen? Will gaming establishments around the globe go belly-up? Will pit bosses, as we know them, cease to exist?

It's all up to you. Employ my tactics for winning, and Vegas is history.

Think you've got the mental resolve to pull it off? Let me warn you: Only those with the strongest self-control can avoid being seduced by the hypnotic allure of the casino and the enticing promises of Lady Luck. In fact, if you love gambling as much as I do, it might well be the most difficult thing you'll ever do. Trust me on this one; even I don't follow my own advice all the time. That's right! I have experienced mental meltdown in the grip of casino fever—have surrendered my winning edge under the influence of gambling's hypnotic spell. But, then again, when I *do* practice what I preach, I win more often than I lose.

So can you.

The Challenge

You don't have to be the typical psyched-out, tapped-out gambler. Learning and *using* the tactics I present in this book will make you the kind of player casino managers fear the most; the kind of player they call *"tough"*; the kind of player who knows how to win. If you're a first-time visitor to a gaming destination, these tactics will help you avoid the casino traps that will most certainly ambush your bankroll. If you're a regular casino visitor, these tactics will help you win more or lose less than you have in the past.

Please understand that these tactics didn't materialize overnight, nor did they come cheaply. They were formulated during three decades of casino play, a time when I lost many, many thousands of dollars making every gambling mistake known to man! The tactics were developed as my first line of defense against making those mistakes again.

I challenge you to learn and use these tactics to become a *tough* player, a *winning* player. At first you might feel the tactics are limiting your gambling spontaneity and putting undue restrictions on your action. Don't despair—these feelings will pass. In fact, once you start reaping the benefits that come from employing the tactics, you will enjoy your gambling more than ever. It's a lot like getting in good physical shape: The longer you work at it, the easier and more rewarding it becomes.

Do you need to follow *every* tactic *every* time you play in a casino?

Yes.

Will you do it?

Probably not.

But don't get discouraged if you slip up once in a while. It is better to practice even one of the tactics some of the time than none of the tactics all of the time! Remember, the more tactics you use—and the more often you use them—the more success you'll enjoy in the casino.

Is it worth the effort? Definitely, if you'd rather be making withdrawals than deposits at the casino. Yes, also, if you are interested in developing the kind of *character* that separates winners from losers not only in casinos, but in all of life's little games.

Emerging victorious in the battle against the casino is important for all of us. It gives us the winning edge not only at the tables, but at any activity requiring us to harness our psychobiological powers. As strange as it may seem, a casino is an excellent place to develop both mental and physical resolve, to learn psychological *and* biological self-control under fire. After all, if you can resist the temptations of an Atlantic City or Monte Carlo, what mountain can't you climb?

A Word Of Caution

Some of you, upon reading this book, will learn you're the type of gambler who *cannot* win in the casino. You have the kind of psychobiological temperament that precludes you from playing in a winning manner. In lay terms, you are an "on-tilt," compulsive gambler... and if this book helps you identify and deal appropriately with your affliction, then my writing time will have been well-spent.

This book is about winning. It's about using new skills to overcome the opposition and come out on top. In the casino as well as in life, you don't want to make a wager if you can't bet on yourself first... and win.

CHAPTER 2

Do You Know
Why You Gamble?

I wouldn't be much of a university professor if I didn't give you a test. So grab a pencil, find a quiet place, and please answer the question below. Please provide a thoughtful, honest response. If you do, you'll be in a better position to use the strategy in this book most effectively. You can write your answer in the box I've provided or just keep it in your mind; either way, please don't turn the page until you've finished the assignment.

"Why do you gamble in a casino?"

All right, time to check your answer. Is this what you wrote down?

> "I gamble in a casino to lose money."

I certainly hope not.
Well, then, maybe you answered this way:

> "I gamble in a casino to win money."

I certainly hope so.
Now, here comes the zinger... hang on to your seat. If you're like 95 percent of the gamblers visiting casinos today, *both* of the answers are true for you!
"How can this be?" you ask.
Because your gambling *intentions* and your gambling *actions* are at cross-purposes. Your intention is to gamble in a casino to win money; but your action—the *way* you gamble in a casino—is to lose money.
Put another way:

> "The *reason* I gamble in a casino is to win money."

> "The *way* I gamble in a casino is to lose money."

Perhaps you don't believe me, or at least you don't count yourself among the 95 percent of gamblers who play in a manner that loses money. If you think your *winning intentions* and *betting action* match, then consider this:

If your major (or only) reason for gambling in a casino is to win money, then you must restrict your play to those activities where your skill and the house rules combine to provide you with a long-term positive expectation of financial gain. This limits you to dog or horse racing, sports betting, and live poker where you must be good enough to beat the other players and overcome the house *take*, referred to as a *rake* at the poker tables, a *take out* at the track, and a *vig* in the sports book. These terms refer to the profits taken by the house as a percentage of bets (the house doesn't bank the bets; it simply runs the games). Arguably, we could also add certain casino-banked games such as blackjack and some types of progressive slot machines to the list. Be forewarned, however, that only the most skilled and disciplined players can expect to show a long-term profit from these casino wagers.

"But wait!" you exclaim, "what about baccarat? And craps... I like to play dice!"

Well, now you've got a problem. Roulette, dice, keno, baccarat, the money wheel, and most slot machines are "negative expectation" games and, in the long run, there is no legal way you can realize a profit from wagering on them.

That's right, dear reader... I said *no way!*

Not with a "system."

Not by wearing your lucky corduroy jacket.

Not by letting a virgin roll the dice.

Not even by living a noble life and giving generously to the charity of your choice.

Here is the sobering reality you must face: If you choose to play _any_ casino game where the house has the odds in its favor—you are going to end up losing in the long run. Period. _Finis_. End of argument.

"Wait a minute," you argue, "I might not win _in the long run_ but what about the short run?"

That will take an amendment in your reason for gambling in the casino. It will now read:

> "I gamble in a casino to win money in the short run."

Ahhh, the short run. OK. If you want to gamble and make a profit from a negative expectation game _in the short run_ then your short-run strategy becomes, well, incredibly short! What you want to do is take _all_ the money you ever intend to gamble, go to the casino of your choice, place it on the lowest house-advantage wager you can find, and await the outcome. (Obviously, I'm not telling you to actually go out and do this. I'm only telling you that it makes great sense in theory, but it does have its practical shortcomings.)

If you lose... well, so much for your gambling career. At least you have the satisfaction of knowing you gave yourself the best mathematical shot at the casino bankroll. If you win, you should take the money and run, because any further bets will decrease your mathematical expectation for maximum profit.

"Hey, hold on there," you counter. "What fun is it to go all the way to the casino to place one bet? Of course I want to win, but I also want to play."

Now we're beginning to see that the reason a person gambles in a casino might not be so simple and straightforward as he or she first believed. I'm going to amend your reason for gambling once again to reflect your latest requirements.

> "I gamble in a casino to win money and to play."

Now you have two reasons to gamble in a casino. They both sound reasonable enough on the surface. The only problem is these two gambling goals are mutually exclusive! **In any casino game where the percentage favors the house, the greater the number of wagers you make, the greater the chances become for the casino to win your money.** Of course, the more wagers you make, the more time it will take for this to happen. Therein lies the rub:

If you want the best possible chance of making a profit playing a negative expectation game, then you should make one bet with your total bankroll. On the other hand, if you want the longest possible time to play at the tables, you should break your bankroll into as many bets as possible. (But remember what I said about the practical aspects of this advice. I've presented it here purely for illustration.)

What's your preference: more time at the tables or more money in your pocket? Most players will probably want both (no wonder some people think gamblers are wacky).

In Section Six, Chapter 17, I'll present you with a betting strategy aimed at giving you a chance for both action *and* short-term profits at the tables. By necessity, it is a "middle ground" strategy—it *won't* give you the best chance for short-term winning, nor will it give you the best chance of staying the longest possible time at the tables. *What it will give you is a reasonable chance of winning in the short run with a reasonable amount of playing time*. Because that is, in the final analysis, what most people really want out of gambling when they play negative expectation games.

Which brings me to a final observation for this chapter. There are some gamblers who really don't worry that much about winning *or* losing in the casino. For them, the *act* of gambling—and the pleasure it brings—is more important than whether they win or lose money in the process. If they were to be accurate in responding to the test question at the front of this chapter, their answer should have read:

> "I gamble in a casino to play."

The sad truth is that many players view the casino as an adult theme park, with their gambling stake being the price they pay to be taken for a ride! **They pay to play rather than play to win.** Such players often express the view that losing money is an acceptable price to pay for their casino "entertainment." They make comments like: "I'd spend this kind of money on a good meal and a show... what's the difference?" or "It's the price I'm willing to pay for having a good time." One punter put it this

odd-even, where the *"en prison"* feature applies and drops
the house edge to an acceptable 1.35 percent. Some American casinos, however, are considering *en prison* as a way
to perk up the game.

Casino managers don't fear the person who gambles to
play; they fear the person who gambles to win. I want
casino mangers to fear *you*, and I want *you* to win. Following the recommendations in this chapter will get you
headed in the right direction. Beware, however, that the
casino operators aren't going to let you win without a
struggle. They've designed their gaming establishments
to make winning difficult and losing very, very easy. How
you can counter their tactics and use the casino on your
terms is the subject-matter of the next chapter.

**The only legal way to gain a money-winning
edge over the casino is to restrict your play
to those activities where your skill and the
house rules combine to provide you with a
long-term *positive expectation* of financial
gain.**

**If you are a player who insists on playing
negative-expectation games, restrict your
action to those games and wagers where
the house advantage doesn't exceed 1.6
percent. Making bets that carry a higher
casino edge will decrease your chances of
winning in the short run and increase the
size of your losses in the long run.**

SECTION TWO

The Two Things You Need to Know About Casinos: How They Use You; How You Can Use Them!

Think of the casino as a giant spider web. The only question is: Are you the spider or the fly?

Linda Thomas
Professional Blackjack Player

CHAPTER 3

How Casinos Are Designed To Make You Lose

In the past quarter-century, I have witnessed some really wild, weird, wonderful, and woeful incidents in casinos throughout the world. Let me share with you my favorite one. This incident isn't fiction. I was there and saw it happen:

Las Vegas On $60,000 A Day

It was my second day on a junket and things weren't going my way. I was in a posh casino on the Las Vegas Strip, exhorting two plastic cubes to come up with the point-number 5. They weren't listening. "Seven... line away, pay the don'ts," intoned the stickman, and a sure-fingered dealer whisked my chips off the green baize layout.

It was then that Mr. C made his appearance at the table. He was wearing an old pair of dirty pants and a denim work shirt and, as he edged up to the rail, he looked like an auto mechanic ready to shoot a little craps on his lunch break. He took some crumpled bills from his shirt pocket and called for twenty nickel ($5.00) chips. The stickman shoved six dice in his direction and announced: "New shooter coming out." I eyed the unkempt Mr. C and decided he looked as frayed as my bankroll. I took it as a sign and decided it was time to take a break.

A few hours later, I was walking past the casino when I heard the unmistakable clamor of dice players at a hot table. A winning table is a noisy table... and a crowded one. Players shout out bets and cheer the shooter, while spectators push and shove to catch a glimpse of the game. By the time I reached the scene, people were stacked up three-deep around the table, and I had to strain my neck just to see the action. It was a big game. Lots of black ($100) chips dotted the layout. The players were hunched over the table like hungry wolves over a freshly killed carcass; now, however, they were feasting on the casino's chips, frantically doled out by harried dealers as number after number kept showing on the dice.

And who was at the center of all the tumult? None other than the slovenly Mr. C. This time, however, I hardly noticed his attire; far more imposing was the tray full of black chips in front of him. It was hard to believe. There must have been $20,000 there!

I watched Mr. C play. He was a *"desperado"*—a gambler's term for a player who likes to bet fast and hard. When a good hand shows, a *desperado* can take the casino for a bundle. When the dice are cold... well, a *desperado* can lose *el pronto*.

The dice stayed hot. Mr. C ran out of rail space to store his chips, and he began stuffing the overflow in his two shirt pockets. As the dice kept passing, he began to bulge noticeably in the chest area, giving him the appearance of a female impersonator with a lumpy bra. It was really quite comical, but nobody was laughing, particularly the pit boss who realized the padding represented about $10,000 worth of house money.

I observed the game a while more, until the dice started chopping, and players drifted from the table. Mr. C showed no signs of quitting, and I wondered if he'd have the good sense to pull in his horns and take down a profit. I made a mental note to check back at the tables after I took in dinner and a show.

The next time I saw Mr. C was five hours later. He was still at the same craps table, tossing black chips onto the layout from a stack he kept cupped in his right hand. His shirt pockets were still stuffed, and now there were significant bulges in his pants pockets as well. Mr. C was literally bloated with casino chips... and his gluttony was not going unnoticed. A security guard kept a knot of curious onlookers a respectable distance from the table, while several floorpersons and the shift boss watched the action from the dice pit.

I wondered about Mr. C's endurance... and his luck. Could either hold out much longer? I overheard a boxman tell a dealer that Mr. C had been going nonstop for over nine hours. All that action at high stakes can do funny things to a person's head. I took a closer look. Mr. C's movements had slowed a bit and he was drinking steadily; still, he didn't look like a man about to call it a night. I remembered Einstein's observation about God playing dice with the universe and wondered if He had designated Mr. C to be the shooter.

Morning is always too early in Las Vegas. I woke up around 11:30 and decided a good deli lunch would shake yesterday's cobwebs from my mind. I was on my way to the restaurant when I spotted Mr. C standing next to his suitcase, just a few feet inside the hotel entrance. He was still wearing the same dirty clothes, but his face looked different. There was a strangeness in his eyes. I wondered what had happened.

"You know him?"

The voice caught me by surprise. It was a hotel bellman who had helped me with my bags on several occasions. "Do you know him?" the bellman repeated.

"Not really. I saw him gambling yesterday," I answered.

"Did you hear what happened to him?"

"No. I was just wondering about that."

The bellman shook his head. "He was winning a lot of money..."

"I know... must've been $40,000."

"More like sixty. They had to send out the racks to get the chips to the cage."

"He cashed in?"

"Nope. Safekeeping. When he got to $60,000 he decided to take a break."

"To his room?"

"That's the real joke. He didn't *have* a room. He was a drifter, passing through"

"No job?"

"He said he was a pipefitter from Chicago, going to LA to find work. He stopped off in Vegas as a lark."

"He must've had some money," I interjected, "I saw him buy in for a hundred at the tables."

"That was his whole bankroll... the last hundred bucks to his name."

"You sure?"

"Absolutely," the bellman replied. "He built a toothpick into a lumberyard."

"That's pretty hard to believe," I said.

"If you think that's hard, listen to this!" The bellman waved his arms with a flourish. "When the shift boss found out the guy didn't have a room, they gave him a penthouse suite... sent him right up."

"One suitcase and all?" I asked wryly.

"That's not all they sent up there." The bellman gave me a wink.

"Looks like the management didn't want to see Mr. C abscond with his winnings."

"No way," the bellman agreed.

"Go on."

"Around eight o'clock the guy wakes up and staggers down to the casino. He's still got a hangover and he's walking bowlegged... but he remembers that money and he wants some heavy action. The swing shift was alerted and waiting for him—opened up a new table... the works."

"And he started betting fast and heavy..."

"He couldn't get it down fast enough. He was covering all the numbers and taking the field at a thousand a pop."

"I know... I watched him yesterday."

"Well, yesterday the dice were passing... this morning they weren't."

"Did anyone ever tell you you're quite a philosopher?" I said sarcastically, looking first at the bellman and then at Mr. C still camped near the doorway. "How long did it take to break him?"

"About an hour. He ran through every cent he had. When he was tapped-out they got his bag from the suite, gave him some walking money, and told him to hit the road."

"Did he say anything to anybody?"

"What's there to say?" the bellman wondered, shrugging his shoulders. "The man lost $60,000 in an hour. That says it all."

In a way, my bellman friend was right. What else *could* one say? An unemployed construction worker loses 60 thousand in 60 minutes... certainly more money than he'll ever *make* in an hour. It's enough to scramble a person's brain. It must have scrambled mine, because suddenly I felt compelled to approach Mr. C and solicit his thoughts on the matter.

I walked over to where he was standing. "Excuse me..." I said awkwardly, not knowing exactly how to begin. "...Weren't you the guy I saw winning at the tables yesterday?"

Mr. C turned and faced me directly. "Yes. But I lost it all back." There was no rancor in his voice, not even a hint of disappointment. He sounded matter-of-fact, like some person recounting a day at the office.

"*All* of it? You must have been winning thousands of dollars."

"All of it... $62,500 to be exact."

I couldn't understand how he could be so nonchalant. "My God, man! What happened? Why didn't you put some of it away?"

Mr. C stared at me with his strange blue eyes. They were wide and unmoving. "I wanted action."

Something about that response irritated me, and I snapped back: "Action? But for what? Now you have zero! You have nothing to show for it!"

My outburst didn't seem to have any effect. "You're wrong," he countered. "I do have something to show for it."

"Oh, yeah? What?"

"Memories." A wisp of a smile played across Mr. C's face. "I've got memories to show for it." And without a further word, the unemployed pipefitter from Chicago picked up his suitcase, walked out the hotel door, and disappeared into the simmering heat of the Las Vegas afternoon.

Beyond "The Jaws Of Averages."

Let me guess what you're thinking. You're thinking that Mr. C was crazy. "How could anybody be so stupid?" you wonder. Well, consider this: Every year millions of casino visitors lose billions of dollars at the tables and the slots. They, too, walk away, cherishing the memories of their trip while seemingly oblivious to the carnage enacted upon their bankrolls. Granted, most of them didn't gamble as high or recklessly as Mr. C, but they *did* lose and they *did* leave, savoring fond memories. Most can't wait to return for another plucking. Why?

Because the "marks" were "cooled out." That's conman jargon for saying that the visiting gamblers (marks) were separated from their funds in a manner that left them feeling satisfied with the outcome (cooled out). Remember how Tom Sawyer got all those neighborhood kids to whitewash his fence? Those kids even paid him to do it, because he psyched them into believing it was an enjoyable job. Now *that* was cooling out the mark. The pharmaceutical company that produces cherry-flavored cough syrup also understands the importance of cooling out the mark. And the casino operator who creates an environment that makes losers feel like winners does, too.

Which brings us to a fine irony. Every day, gamblers from all over the world hit the tables and slots in search of the golden fleece... and every day, most of them return home—victims of a golden fleecing. The fleece-seeker has become the fleeced with nary a whimper, bedazzled by the casino operators "sleight-of-mind."

Sound ridiculous? Believe me, it isn't! Casinos have been skillfully designed to mollify losers—to cool them out and make them feel their losses were worth it. That these losers keep coming back is proof-positive casinos work.

Of course, to keep losers coming back, one must have losers in the first place. To stimulate losing, casinos create an attraction—a tractor beam, if you will—to draw people to the tables, keep them there and encourage reckless, high-risk gambling... all of which encourages "splurging" rather than saving, losing rather than winning.

> The casino is a highly sophisticated money
> trap, created for one purpose: to separate you
> from your bankroll with elegance, efficiency,
> and elan. It is not a place to let down your guard
> and relax. You are at war against a formidable
> foe and you're fighting on your adversary's
> home turf.

Well, then, what about you, the player who wants a
gambling chance of winning in the casino? Your goal
should be to turn the tables on the casino operators: to
beat them at their own psychological games and gain that
all-important mental edge during play. To do this you
first need to know about the casino ploys designed to
make you a loser. Simply understanding what these ploys
are—and how they work—will put you in a better position to fight and overcome them. Then you'll be ready to
take the offensive and learn how to *use the casino* to
enhance your winning chances in the games you choose
to play.

One timely warning before we begin: Learning to use
(rather than be used by) casinos will be no easy task.
Casino operators are skilled practical psychologists. They
understand every nuance of human emotion and weakness; they know every psychological trick to get you to
turn your pants pockets inside out—the gambler's white
flag of surrender. Yet, with knowledge and resolve, you
can prevail at the tables—and you *must*—if you want to
build profits rather than casinos on your future gambling
trips.

The Strange Case Of The
One-Way Walkway

Caesars Palace is a deluxe hotel-casino on the Strip, aglow like a giant blue ice cube in the Las Vegas night. Let me tell you an interesting story about this place:

If you've ever been to the "Palace," you know it is set back from one of the busiest intersections on the Strip. It is several hundred feet from the street to the casino door. Now, several hundred feet might not seem like a long distance to travel... but in Vegas, people have been known to evaporate walking from their hotel room to the swimming pool! At any rate, Caesars has constructed a rainbow-shaped "skyway," complete with a moving walkway, to whisk gamblers from the Strip intersection right to the front door of the hotel.

Many years ago I decided to try out the skyway. It was fun. As the trip progressed, a recorded voice described all the great pleasures awaiting me as an honored guest of Caesar himself. Well, that was pretty heady stuff... and by the time I hit the end of the walkway, I was ready to participate in all sorts of debauchery.

I stayed at the Palace for several hours, then decided to visit some downtown casinos. I stepped outside and looked for the return skyway. There wasn't one. Anywhere. I finally checked with the doorman. "We bring them in, but we don't take them out," was his reply.

The one-way walkway at Caesars Palace is important because it tells us something about the casino operators and how they think.

It turns out that their guiding principle is to *attract people into their casinos and keep them there*. Or, as one hotel executive quipped, "Get 'em in and keep 'em in." And that is *exactly* what the one-way walkway was built to accomplish. Caesars Palace is happy to provide an expensive transport that will make your access to the casino both easy and attractive. But leaving—well, that's a horse of a different color. At that point you're on your own. Meanwhile, the casino operators can always hope that once you leave their air-conditioned hotel and realize you have to walk back to Las Vegas Boulevard, you'll turn around and head back into their casino.

> **The casino operator's prime directive is to get you into the casino and keep you there as long as possible. Think of casinos as spider webs that have been designed, embellished, and strategically placed to catch and hold prey. Make sure you don't get stuck in the web... figuratively or financially.**

"Get 'em in and keep 'em in." Now that you're aware of what the casino operator is trying to accomplish, a whole lot of things about gaming establishments begin to make sense. For instance:

The Casino As A Focal Point

Consider, for a moment, the orb-weaving spider. This little creature spins a web to snare its prey. Some spiders are smarter than others. The clever ones spin their webs in places where passing meals are more likely to fly by—like around outdoor lights. After all, the better the traffic flow, the better the menu.

Owners of gaming establishments build webs, too. Their webs are called "casinos" (guess what role *you* play). And, like the clever spider, they build their webs where traffic density is high. But, whereas the spider can't alter its environment to "draw more customers" into its web (it might search for an outdoor light, but it can't build one), a casino operator can... and does. This is why many casino hotels have been designed to funnel more people into their gaming areas. Want some examples?

ITEM: In many hotels, you have to pass through, or along the edge of the casino to get to the front desk.

ITEM: If you want to cash any travelers checks, you are often directed to the casino cage, rather than to the hotel cashier.

ITEM: Getting to and from most shows requires a trip through (or near) the casino. And while you're waiting to enter the showroom... guess where they have you line up.

ITEM: Spiders build their webs near bright lights because doing so attracts more "customers" at night. Ever notice the candlepower near a casino entrance? Enough to make a spider lick its mandibles.

Oftentimes, the entire design and placement of hotel facilities are geared to get people into the casino, not to mention the intriguing facade, or themed attraction in front of the casino.

Nobody should underestimate the importance of the "casino as a focal point" concept. This cleaver ruse also increases the impact of **impulse gambling...** the type of play that encourages losing rather than winning at the tables. Many players, especially tourists, will decide to play even though they had no intention of doing so at the outset. The lure of the games everywhere they turned was too much to resist.

I'm sure you've heard stories about people who ended up gambling because they passed a casino while on their way to somewhere else. Such stories seldom have happy endings. In fact, some of the most memorable tales in gambling folklore attest to the effectiveness of placing casinos at the crossroads to everywhere.

Take, for example, the story of the well-known comedian Joe E. Lewis. It seems he was on a dinner date at a casino's gourmet restaurant when his companion asked for some cigarettes. He excused himself from the table and walked to the lobby newsstand to get a pack. The newsstand, of course, was at the opposite side of the casino. Lewis liked to gamble. A few minutes later he returned and the meal was completed without further interruption. Later, as he prepared to leave the restaurant, he noticed his lady friend had left the cigarettes on the table.

"Better take the cigarettes with you, honey," he suggested, "they cost me $32,000."

And Lewis, the comedian, wasn't joking.

Embellishing The Web

The casino owners know their livelihoods depend on gaming revenue. They also know that in the long run a certain proportion of all monies wagered will end up in their coffers. Thus, they have made their casinos the focal point of hotel complexes and—in some cases like Las Vegas—the centerpoint of entire cities, in hopes of getting more action at the tables. And they haven't stopped there. They've even "one-upped" our orb-weaving spider by developing a better web.

A spider's web is inconspicuous and does nothing to entice any prey that happens by. Not so with a casino. The gaming establishment is very carefully designed as a lure, embellished with all kinds of goodies to make it more attractive and irresistible.

Take, as a case in point, the give-aways and drawings that are available in gaming locales throughout the United States. Where are they held? In the casino. You must enter the web to win. There are lounge shows and bars in almost every casino as well, with the music and liquor doing their share of bringing visitors into the web. Then, too, there are shills. The shills are usually attractive women who sit at the gaming tables, adding their physical allure to an already compelling environment. And, most importantly, there are the amplified sounds of winning: slot tokens clanking into metal bowls... sounds that summon gamblers to the casino as surely as bells call the devoted to Sunday worship.

There are not many individuals who can stand outside this web and resist falling prey to the temptations just a few steps away. Which brings us to another friendly casino strategy:

Getting Customers To "Stick" Around The Casino

Spiders spin sticky webs to keep their "guests" in place. Casino operators use the same approach, figuring that the longer they *keep* you in their establishments, the longer you might gamble and lose.

Keeping people in casinos is not that difficult—particularly in gambling locations where there aren't a lot of other activities taking place. Then, too, the lures that drew people to the casino in the first place—money, drink, music, etc.—can also help hold them there. In addition, the casino operators provide extra "adhesives" once you enter their establishments. For instance, they dangle "fun books" that offer free rolls of quarters, two-for-one play at various table games, even souvenirs. The hitch? You have to check in every hour at a casino booth to redeem your coupons. It is literally impossible to leave the casino and still use the books. So you stay in the web.

The casino management also makes sure there are no clocks around to remind the player of any other commitments. Time is literally suspended in the casinos. Consider, too, that many casinos never close, so there is no time limit requiring the casinos to arbitrarily cut off play (who ever heard of a spider turning out a fly because it was closing time!).

Gambling: The Ultimate Adhesive

When it comes to keeping people in the casino web, nothing beats gambling itself. Once people start playing, it's hard for them to stop—at least while money is still available to put into action. It is this compelling, addictive aspect of gambling that makes it the single most powerful adhesive for keeping you in the casino.

Furthermore, **for many casino patrons the very act of gambling is so arousing that it makes reasoned judgment and self control very difficult, if not impossible.** For these players, the stimulation from gambling is so intense that their performance—along with their mental resolve—deteriorates, leaving them ill-prepared to deal logically and skillfully in the casino. Like a moth attracted to the flame or metal filings pulled to the magnet, these gamblers are drawn to the casino and stuck there... unable to break free although their money, their dignity, or even their lives may be at stake. If you doubt the potent lure of gambling, consider these *true* stories:

ITEM: A fire burned through part of a large Vegas hotel. Even as smoke curled through the casino, gamblers were reluctant to leave. The slot players were a particular problem. One woman steadfastly refused to vacate her machine, and she had to be carried bodily from the burning building.

ITEM: Years ago there was a flash flood that roared through the streets of Las Vegas. Water surged into the casino at Caesars Palace and stood several feet deep in places. It didn't stop the gamblers. They just rolled up their pants and kept on playing.

ITEM: A friend of mine was shooting dice. He had been playing for several hours when he felt the urge to visit the bathroom. Just then the dice turned hot. They stayed that way. My friend had a choice: stay on the hot roll and defecate in his pants; or go to the bathroom and interrupt his winning streak. It was no contest. He crapped in his pants. Now I know how the game got its name.

ITEM: A man collapsed while shooting craps. He was laid out on the casino carpet, in full view of the other players, to await assistance. The game never stopped for a moment. When the player was revived, his first words were: "Did I make my point?"

Now, let me make *my* point. The people in the stories I have just recounted were *not* hard-core, degenerate gamblers. They were players... players a lot like you and me. Yet, caught up in the fever-pitch of gambling, they did some very strange things. And some not-so-very-strange-things—like losing money. Why? Because they succumbed to the casino's temptations. But you won't, will you?

Stimulus Bombardment

Casino operators aren't satisfied simply getting you into the casino and keeping you there, they also try to reduce your gambling effectiveness through the use of "stimulus bombardment."

Ever wonder why casino operators lobby to keep their gaming establishments open 24 hours a day? After all, it costs plenty to keep three shifts of employees on the job.

Is it done as a convenience for locals who might want a late-night dinner?

No.

Is it done to accommodate visitors who arrive after work?

No.

What about as a service to insomniacs?

Wrong!

Gaming establishments have been designed and staffed for 24-hour operation because the casino operators—those masters of human psychology—are fully aware that non-stop, round-the-clock action is a most effective way to separate players from their bankroll in the least possible time.

In explaining why this is so, we need to understand the impact of stimulus bombardment and how it is used to raise players' arousal levels to a point where their performance in the casino is compromised.

Anyone who has ever been to a large casino or a gambling town like Las Vegas will know all about "stimulus bombardment."

It occurs when a person is confronted with more sights and sounds—for longer, continuous periods of time—than he or she is used to handling. Like walking down the Strip with its neon dazzle, or stepping into a casino amidst the din of crapshooters, the pulsing rhythm of amplified music, and the staccato racket of slot tokens hitting the paybowls like hailstones hammering a tin roof.

In Las Vegas, stimulus bombardment is a way of life and it cannot be avoided. This is because, as author Tom Wolfe notes, "...Las Vegas has succeeded in wiring an entire city with this electronic stimulation, day and night, out in the middle of the desert."

What happens when you are subjected to this constant stimulus bombardment? Scientists know—and so do casino operators. You begin to think and act differently. Rational thought becomes more irrational. You become more emotional and impulsive. Normal defenses and inhibitions seem to melt away. Do you know what that adds up to at the tables?

Profits.

For the casinos.

A successful casino is designed as a giant pep pill—a kind of electrical jolt created to course through your body and keep you charged up for non-stop revelry and gambling. There are no clocks on the walls to tell you it's late, no windows to remind you that the sun has set.

If you're lucky you'll experience "casino burnout" once you return home, moping around for days like a person coming down from amphetamines.

If you're *not* lucky, you'll begin to experience burnout while you're still *in* the casino. The problem is you probably won't notice the symptoms: the reduced concentration, the poorer judgment, the sloppier and more aggressive betting. You'll be too psyched up by the casino energy to notice. It's similar to the football player who cracks a rib during play, but is so high on the game he doesn't feel pain until the final gun sounds.

One thing you will notice, however, is the price you've paid for your folly. Gambling is a very exhausting activity, particularly if you're trying to count cards at the black-jack table, decide what to keep or toss out in video poker, or track several bets at craps or roulette. Action is the name of the game in the casino, and it comes fast and furious.

If you don't learn to pace yourself in this animated environment, your skills and your bankroll will suffer. The casino operators realize this and do what they can to keep you hyped up and going at a frenetic pace. You must learn to resist these tactics; otherwise you might end up like the diver who, bedazzled by the beauty of the deep, suddenly realizes he has run out of air.

The Secret Behind The Curtain

While we're on the topic of stimulus bombardment, let's take a stroll down the fabled Las Vegas Strip... and don't forget your sunglasses! There you will see, in a rainbow burst of neon, the names of well-known enter-tainers—show business superstars who are making per-sonal appearances in packed hotel showrooms. And they aren't the only audience-pleasers in town. There are thou-sands of other performers who participate in the various production shows: musicals, variety galas, ice reviews, water reviews, anatomical reviews... you name it. No wonder Las Vegas bills itself as the "Live Entertainment Capital of the World." It is a well-deserved title. It seems that every hotel-casino in Vegas—*and almost every major casino worldwide*—offers some kind of showroom enter-tainment for its patrons.

Now I've got a question for you: *Why* all these shows in the first place? What *purpose* is served by this avalanche of entertainment?

"To attract visitors," you say.

"True," I respond.

"...And to get them in the vicinity of the casino," you add.

"Also true," I agree. These are two of the reasons that showroom entertainment exists in Vegas and other casino locations. But there is also a *third* reason for all this entertainment... and this reason is often unknown to the player: a kind of secret lurking behind the showroom curtain. *What is this third reason?* Let me tell you by way of a personal story.

Back in the early days of my gambling—before I had developed my tactics for handling casinos—I was on a junket to Vegas. It was my second night in town. I had been gambling the better part of 30 hours. I was exhausted. My play in the casino was deteriorating, and so was my bankroll. I did the smart thing. I decided to quit for the night. I was only down a little, in striking distance of turning things around.

Because it was only 9 p.m., one of my buddies suggested we catch a show and unwind. It seemed like a good suggestion. I hadn't really gotten into the show scene and I thought it would be a novel way to relax and pass the few hours until bedtime. Was I in for a shock!

The show featured a comedian and a popular rock group. I don't remember the name of either. What I do remember is this: I walked into the show, drained of energy, tired and melancholy over my table losses. By the time the show ended, I was flush with energy, wired for action and totally sure I could beat the tar out of the casino in any game I chose.

I wish I could report a happy ending to this story. I could if I were a casino owner. Sadly, such was not the case. Buoyed by my new sense of energy and confidence, I mounted a full-scale offensive against the casino coffers. I thought I was fresh and ready. One hour later, I was fresh, all right... fresh out of money. And I was ready, too... ready to pack my things. I had blown my entire bankroll... all at a time when I had no business gambling at all.

Which brings me to the third reason casino/hotels sponsor Las Vegas-style entertainment. **It is to encourage gambling by those patrons who might otherwise abstain because of fatigue or discouragement over earlier losses.**

The Vegas-style show has amazing curative powers. The humorous comedians can cure your blues, make you laugh at your misfortunes. The high-energy performers can chase that drowsy feeling, make you wide-eyed and tingling for action.

Did you ever see a *sad* show in Vegas? Ever wonder why not? Look at it this way: Would you feel like gambling after watching some sobering tale of death and misfortune? Of course not! And what of the laborious pace of the opera? Would you feel like hitting the tables after two drinks and *The Flying Dutchman?* I doubt it. Opera, symphony, ballet... the more serious "art" forms don't usually have the kind of optimism and frantic pace that helps maintain the stimulus bombardment desired by the casino operators. The hype isn't there. Neither is the raw humor of the backroom comedian who makes us forget our wounded pride and flattened wallets.

The "Vegas-style" show, then, is just one more part of the casino operator's overall strategy for keeping you up and keeping you gambling. Getting you to spend your money more liberally in the casino is another part of their strategy.

Casinos are designed to encourage freewheeling and plentiful spending by a willing and satisfied clientele. The use of casino chips and credit, the party atmosphere at the tables, the royal treatment afforded players, and the presence of shills are but a few of the casino tactics that make it easier to separate gamblers from their bankrolls.

Currency Devaluation, Casino Style

One way to get people to spend more is by making them think their money is worth less. The casino operators realize this and work hard to make dollars seem less valuable to the wagering player.

My first experience with currency devaluation was a memorable one. I had just entered the Desert Inn for my first go at casino gambling in Las Vegas. I was nervous and excited... I really didn't know what to do or expect. I decided to make some bets in the $1 to $5 range, and see how I would fare. Pulling out my wallet, I made my way

to the cashier's window and handed over five $20 bills—
my total gambling stake—to the lady behind the counter.

"Could I have some change, please?"

The woman didn't blink an eyelash. "Sure," she replied, and handed me back a $100 bill.

Suddenly $20 didn't seem like very much money any-
more.

One of the most successful casino tactics for making
your dollars seem less valuable is the use of chips at the
gaming tables. People tend to forget that the cute little
red, green, or black disks in their hands are, in reality,
$5, $25, and $100 bills. Such memory lapses can be very
costly.

To make matters worse, the dealers refer to the $5 and
$25 chips as "nickel" and "quarter" chips, respectively.
How's that for currency devaluation!

Credit in the casinos also accomplishes this same currency devaluation effect. Playing against a credit line can
be devastating to your financial health when you consider
that the gambler never actually *sees* any cash in his trans-
actions. How easy it becomes to simply say, "I'll take a
thousand more." No need to reach for your wallet and
see what a thousand dollars really looks like. Simply sign
the marker and place your bets. It's so unreal... so much
like playing Monopoly. "Is this really money?" you start
asking yourself.

Believe me, it is.

Creating An Urge To Splurge Through Legitimizing Socially Justified Indulgence

Nothing loosens the purse strings and encourages spending like a carefree party atmosphere. Knowing this, casino operators work hard to give their establishments the aura of perpetual partying, a kind of 365-days-a-year Mardi Gras. This party atmosphere is crucial to legitimizing *socially justified indulgence*. After all, isn't that what a party is all about? Let the good times roll! Eat, drink, and be merry! Life is a cabaret, my friend... so just belly up to the table and put a black chip on the hardways... what the hell, it's *only* money... and besides, it's *fun*.

There's no room for party-poopers in the manufactured gaiety of the casino. Winners are heralded by the ringing of bells and the shouts of the dealers. Drinks and cigarettes are readily available. Nearby a band is playing happy music, and in the showroom there's a comedian to keep you laughing. It's like a birthday party and Christmas holiday all rolled up into one.

By creating gaming establishments that embody a perpetual party atmosphere and legitimizing socially justified indulgence, the casino operators are able to turn social standards upside down. Frugality is held up to ridicule while conspicuous consumption is praised. The casino has been designed to produce a "splurge" mentality in those who visit it... and within its magical walls the spendthrift replaces the skinflint as the hero of the hour.

Feel Like Royalty, Spend Like Royalty

If casino operators were ever to mint a coin of their realm, its face should bear this inscription; *"Every gambler is royalty."* Because that's the way it is in most casinos throughout the world. Where else can a person be treated like a king or queen—afforded front-row everything—simply because he or she is willing to gamble? Being treated like royalty is a great feeling and, as Mario Puzo emphasizes, "...millions of people will lose billions of dollars to taste it."

Instant royalty. The casino operators do everything they can do to make a player feel special, for they know that once people feel like kings and queens, they'll try to spend like kings and queens. Which all means, if you gamble... be prepared to be pampered, spoiled, and generally treated in a manner befitting royalty.

Do not underestimate how "high" this treatment can make you feel... or how quickly it can make you want to throw your money around. Before I learned how to achieve psychobiological control at the tables, that's exactly how I used to react on my Vegas junkets.

I'd arrive at my hotel and waiting for me would be a big basket of fruit and a personal note of welcome from my casino host. Wherever I walked in the hotel, people knew me by my name and treated me with the utmost courtesy and respect. At the gourmet restaurant, I always got the finest service and best food—always at my own special table.

And when I went to gamble, the dealers always made room for me, letting everyone know that I was someone "special." Hell, all I needed was a crown and I figured I could have *ruled* the hotel. Instead, I ended up investing in the place via my craps table losses. I had been "psyched" by the casino hype. I wasn't a king after all... but I had been royally shafted!

Money As Macho

This casino strategy for separating the gambler from his bankroll works primarily with *male* players. The operators of gaming establishments understand the male ego well, and have designed their casinos to take full advantage of it. They know, for example, that many men bet higher and more impulsively in the presence of women because such men equate *money* with *macho*. These men believe that the more they can put on the tables, the more masculine they are.

Tommy Renzoni, the man who brought baccarat to Las Vegas, pegged this male characteristic perfectly when he observed: "Women, it seems to me, have always made a positive difference at a gaming table.... If a beautiful woman is actually playing at a Baccarat table, or in any other game for that matter, time and time again you'll see the activity at the table increase, the number of more substantial bettors grow."

The casino operators have not overlooked this connection between male wagering and female presence. "Every casino I've ever heard of," Renzoni notes, "will have good-looking female employees, shills, sitting at a gaming table playing with house money because they attract male players. They make the room more colorful, beautify it, but basically, they are there as a lure."

Casino owners get rich because they understand the link between a man's ego and his money. They know that when a player is losing (already a blow to his macho image), he'll sometimes use his credit line as a salve to ease his wounded pride; he'll ask for more money to prove his worth. It's almost as if he's saying, "See, I can get a thousand more... I'm worth plenty!" And the casino management is right there to grant his face-saving request.

In his novel, *Las Vegas Strip*, author Morris Renek captures the essence of this credit-line-for-macho strategy. He describes the plight of a gambler, a "Mr. Jackson," who is losing rapidly and signing markers for more chips. The casino boss, "Yank," grants Jackson's requests for money, each time saying "Mr. Jackson is good" for the funds. The effect is stunning:

"'Mr. Jackson is good.' Yank's startling, old-fashioned call was not to be forgotten. The heavier Jackson fell into debt, the deeper was the need for Yank's protective voice. 'Mr. Jackson is good.' Now it was needed like a drug, like fresh air. The words were a simple credit rating, yet they worked as well as any to bear witness that a man was upright. ... 'Mr. Jackson is good.' This declaration upholding his name rolled on through the night until the listeners were mesmerized. It was easy to imagine how fine it would be if one could hear this declaration about oneself. 'Mr. _____ is good.' It would be worth anything to have this said with such authority to a room full of worldly people about your life on this earth."

Money as macho. You can be sure if there is a weakness in human character the casino operators will learn of it and use it to strengthen the house's bottom line. These masters of psychology also use their knowledge of normal human feelings to encourage losing and make winning more difficult to achieve. Thus, they practice a tactic I refer to as:

Love A Loser, Vanquish The Victor

> Casino operators understand the importance of providing comfort and sympathetic support for losing players. Losing players are loved. The *occasional* winner is also treated graciously, but the *steady* winner is a target for scorn and even expulsion from the gaming tables.

Gaming entrepreneurs aren't fools. They understand that happy losers will return to their casinos to lose again. And repeat business is what keeps the lifeblood of a gaming establishment flowing.

Before legalized casino gambling spread across America, Nevada was probably the only state in the country that loved losers. "When you lose, everyone seems so sympathetic and understanding," one player explained to me recently. And why not? Every time the gambler loses, the casino wins, and what business do you know of that doesn't treat its best customers well? One casino manager said it all when he observed: "I never met a loser I didn't like."

The next time you visit a casino, step inside and observe the happy-loser syndrome firsthand. Look around for gamblers who are down on their luck and see how they're treated. Observe the cocktail waitress bringing them free drinks to make them feel better. Listen to the floorman commiserate with them, telling them he's never seen such a streak of bad luck and that things will surely change. Follow the players as they go into the dinner show to be entertained by a comedian who makes them laugh and forget about their slaughtered bankrolls. Watch them leave the showroom and wander outside the casino where the promise of a luckier tomorrow glitters through the neon-sprinkled night.

Nick the Greek, one of the world's most famous gamblers, had an interesting philosophy about gambling. Profit and loss were important to the Greek, but they weren't the end-all of his profession. Even after he'd lost a great deal of money, he'd be quick to emphasize that "…your life doesn't go with it." And that's the way a gambling business wants the player to feel.

"Hey," the casino seems to be saying, "Sure, you might lose, but your life doesn't go with it. So have fun, we love you, and maybe next time you'll beat the tables." Many players seem to agree, losing with smiles on their faces and this kind of comment on their lips: "So what if I lose some money? With all the fun I'm having, it's worth it."

With such attitudes, it's hard to convince happy losers that they are, in fact, losers. They've been psyched into accepting their financial debacle in a positive light. Nor are these attitudes likely to change when you consider how *winners* are treated in casinos. You see, it's not nearly as much fun being a winner—particularly a *consistent winner*—in gaming establishments. Casino operators don't look fondly upon these steady winners, and they reveal their feelings in no uncertain terms.

Some people will argue that casinos love winners. This is simply not true. Casino operators love the *publicity* that winners generate, but don't let that fool you. The occasional winner is touted, but the steady winner is given the cold shoulder... and sometimes the door. Don't take my word for it; ask any competent blackjack counter... if you can find one who hasn't been hassled into quitting or barred from casino play.

Actually, when you stop to consider that gambling is a business that profits from players' losses, then the behavior of casino management becomes more understandable. Every business takes steps to survive and prosper, and the gambling business is no exception. There can be only one steady winner in a casino and, from management's point of view, it better not be the player! That is why steady losers are treated better than steady winners—and it's also why players are given casino "comps" (complimentaries) when they gamble.

> Casinos offer their patrons a wide variety of "freebies" or "comps" (complimentaries) ranging from small ticket items (drinks, T-shirts) to first-class, all-expenses-paid junkets. All comps serve the same purpose: to increase the player's gambling losses at the tables.

Casino Comps: The Free Lunch As A Last Meal

Here's a "free lunch" story to top them all. The manager of a well-known Vegas showroom entertainer had a weakness when it came to freebies. He liked them... a lot. One day the casino offered him four roasted turkeys, on the house. He accepted, gladly. While he waited for the kitchen staff to wrap up his four birds, he wandered over to the craps tables. Suffice it to say he wasn't very lucky that day. His losses were such that, by the time he picked up his "free lunch," each turkey had cost him a cool $25,000!

Sounds like one turkey ended up with four turkeys! But don't be too critical of this gambler. Many everyday gamblers are seduced into losing by casino freebies—and that's exactly why casino operators give them away.

The Year-Round Santa

Here's an incredible little item of interest: A few premium properties give away so many freebies, they have to hire a special employee to distribute the goodies. These employees are called, appropriately, *casino hosts*. Their job? To draw high-rolling gamblers to the casino and develop them into steady, loyal customers.

The casino host is an "ambassador of goodwill" ...an individual who wants to make gamblers feel good about the hotel and casino where they might lose thousands, even millions, of dollars yearly. The host is something of a cross between a genie and Santa Claus, granting wishes and bearing gifts to those gamblers the casino favors.

And what gifts! One host gives his best customers gold money clips, each with a negotiable, black ($100) casino chip inside. Another makes sure that the spouses of valued gamblers are showered with gifts... clothes, sports equipment, jewelry—you name it. Casino hosts also arrange any activities gamblers desire. These might include tickets to a sold-out fight, a round of golf at a championship course, or setting up a trip to a local tourist attraction.

Why are these hosts so nice? Because they want your business. And not just once... but time and time again. A loyal gambler—particularly the high stakes variety—is the biggest asset any casino can have. Hosts are also nice to the players for another reason: They make gambling losses easier to swallow and winnings more difficult to achieve. After all, if you're going to lose, you might as well lose to people you like, right? And if you're going to win, you don't want to win money from people you like, right? "Cushion the losses and limit the wins." That's the motto of your amiable casino host.

The Bottom Line On Casino Freebies

There are many different kinds of freebies offered by casinos throughout the world. But, whether they be free drinks at the tables, an all-expenses-paid junket, or a token of friendship from a casino host, all comps serve the same functions: **(1) to get you gambling and keep you gambling and (2) to encourage poor gambling in the form of (a) showoff gambling; (b) gambling where you lose to "pay back" the freebies; and (c) gambling where**

you hesitate to win big because you feel guilty taking money from the comp-givers.

The casino operators aren't philanthropists, and they certainly aren't dumb. When they "give away" money it's for a reason: to get more money in return. Casino management views comps as investments—as sensible ways to stimulate business and increase profits.

There is an old saying you've all heard: "There's no such thing as a free lunch." That's true in the casino, too. For those of you who might want to partake of the free meal, be careful, or you might end up with your just desserts.

I hope that the material I have presented thus far has convinced you that casino operators have developed a powerful strategy designed to make you a loser at the tables. Before I show you how to counter these tactics and enhance your winning chances, let me mention one additional tactic casino operators sometimes use to reduce your winning chances at the tables.

Hawking And Hiding The House Edge

Casino operators push their high-percentage bets because it brings them greater profits. They also conceal the house edge when possible, depending on player ignorance to make their tactics work.

If you were a car dealer would you rather sell a high markup car or one with a lower profit margin? If you

were a casino operator, would you want to "sell" your
high house percentage bets or those with a lower margin
of profit? Casinos are in business to make money, thus
the dealers have been instructed and the games designed
to steer you toward making high-percentage wagers.

The craps table provides ample evidence of this casino
strategy. First of all, the best bet for the player isn't even
inscribed on the layout! I'm referring to the "odds" bets,
which can be made once a point-number has been established. These bets pay off at true odds, which means that
neither the casino nor the player has an advantage. The
odds-bet is the ONLY fair wager in the casino. For that
reason it isn't advertised, and *only* knowledgeable gamblers can take advantage of it.

When it comes to *bad* bets for the player, however, it's
a layout of a different color. The wagers with the highest
house percentages are very clearly marked on the table,
and placed in a manner to encourage bets. The proposition bets—financial suicide to any gambler—are promi-
nently positioned in the center of the layout where they
can't be missed. The "field" also takes up a large amount
of space, and it's located directly in front of the player to
make wagering easy and tempting.

If, by chance, the player is blind or oblivious to the
betting temptations beckoning from the green felt, the
friendly stickman is always ready to recommend the bad
(high house percentage) bets. The intelligent player avoids
such suggestions like the plague... but the gambler who
doesn't understand the game is often taken in by this
"carney hustle." Don't blame the stickman for encourag-
ing such poor play. It's his job to hustle for the house—to
hawk bets that have a high casino edge. If the player is

dumb enough to get suckered in... well, whose fault is that? Gambling is a business and the player (customer) should remember the consumer credo: "Let the buyer beware."

Casino operators not only tout their biggest money-maker bets, they also hide their built-in profit when they can. Like, for instance, using the word *"for"* instead of *"to"* in designating payoffs on wagers. That little word change might not seem like much... but the difference in meaning can add up to whopping profits for the house.

Savvy players understand the difference between the *"to"* and *"for"* distinctions on the layout, and they know enough about the games they play to steer clear of the sucker bets so attractively placed on the layouts and "recommended" by the dealers. I hope you are one of those players.

Learn To Walk Through The Web

Throughout this chapter, I've made comparisons between the way casino operators build gaming establishments and the way spiders spin webs. Here's one final point of interest about webs. Certain spiders can walk on them yet not get stuck. The same is true of casino "webs." Some players can walk into and out of the webs as they please. Others get stuck... figuratively and financially.

You want to learn to walk *through* the web. The good news is... you've already taken the first step.

> It's easier to avoid the traps and pitfalls the
> casino operators have prepared for you
> now that you know what their tactics are
> and how they work.

In other words, simply by becoming aware of the tactics being used against you, you'll be better prepared to counter them effectively. You now should see the casino environment for what it is... a carefully manufactured dreamworld designed to separate you from your money. And you should be ready for the casino assault on your bankroll. Now, here are the other steps you'll need to take to beat the casino operators at their own psychological tricks.

> Avoid impulse gambling at all costs.

Remember what happened to Joe E. Lewis? He was the comedian who made a "spur-of-the-moment" decision to gamble while on the way to buy a package of cigarettes. It cost him $32,000.

The story of Mr. Lewis is not that unusual. Many people end up gambling "on impulse"; a decision brought on by coming into contact with the sights and sounds of a casino. Of course, not every person who gambles on impulse will end up losing thousands of dollars, yet the increased danger of losing is there, if for no other reason than the player is not properly prepared to challenge the casino from a state of psychobiological readiness.

Never walk into a gambling establishment on impulse.
You are most likely to end up "spider bait" when you
play in this mode. As already indicated, casino operators
have constructed their emporiums to encourage gambling
"on a whim"—which is often psychologically dangerous.
Thus, you want to avoid this kind of play at the tables or
slots.

That's hard to do in places where casinos surround you
with 24-hour-a-day action. In England, gaming clubs are
not allowed to advertise for members. Gaming by credit
is forbidden. New members must wait 48 hours before
gambling in any club they join. Cabaret acts, live music,
and dancing are not allowed in any gaming club. The
purpose of these laws, as stated by the British, is specifi-
cally to protect people from impulse gambling. Players in
America, unfortunately, are afforded no such protection.
Thus, when it comes to controlling your gambling im-
pulses in the United States, you're on your own.

> Get acclimated to your environment before you
> begin gambling. This is particularly important if
> you've traveled over three hours (land *or* air)
> to your gaming destination.

If there is a casino close to your home, then you needn't
worry about this recommendation. However, for those of
you who are driving or flying a long way to reach your
gambling destination, don't ignore my advice. Getting
acclimated to your new environment is particularly important if you're planning to spend three or more days
there. On longer trips, I recommend you don't gamble at

all on your arrival day, especially if you get in after 3:00 p.m. But if you must have a go of it, at least check into your room and take a nice long shower or a dip in the pool first. Then visit the tables, refreshed and ready to battle the casino on *your* terms.

> **Do not spend too much time gambling in a casino. Two to three one-hour sessions per day is optimal for most people.**

I realize there is a temptation—particularly if you can't visit a casino destination as often as you'd like—to gamble for long stretches at a time. Overcome this temptation. Gambling hour after hour makes you more vulnerable to casino "psych-outs" and financial loss.

To play most effectively, you must be at your psychological and physical peak (as we will see in Chapter 10). There is no way this peak can be sustained in marathon sessions at the tables. The twin forces of fatigue and excitement combine to impair your senses—and your judgment. There is also a tendency to increase the size of your bets during long gambling sessions. Increased bets ward off the onset of boredom or fatigue and keep excitement levels high. They also keep casino profits high.

Want to fight the tendency to stay at the tables or slots too long? The next time you visit the casino, try these suggestions:

1. Make a gambling itinerary and stick to it. Know in advance when (how often, how long) you're going to be in the casinos. Setting aside specific times for gam-

bling will help you combat the tendency to "lose track" of how long you've been playing.

2. Make plans to participate in as many non-gambling activities as needed to fill out your non-gaming hours. That way you won't have time on your hands, get bored, and hit the tables.

3. Wear a watch and be aware of time. Don't let the clockless casinos trick you into gambling too long.

> **Maintain the proper attitude toward—and respect for—the value of money. Beware of the casino tactics that encourage reckless spending through (1) currency devaluation; (2) legitimizing *socially justified indulgence;* (3) treating the gambler like royalty; (4) encouraging the *money as macho* syndrome at the tables; and (5) the distribution of "comps" to players.**

Whenever you are about to buy-in at the tables or take out a marker, always ask yourself two questions: (1) What could I buy for myself or my family with this money?; (2) How long will I have to work to make back this money should I lose it? Asking those questions each time you begin gambling should help keep the value of your money in proper perspective.

Don't gamble to be loved, gamble to win. Casino managers love losers. Remember, you're not out to win their affection, you're out to win their money.

Casino operators design their games to encourage high-percentage play at the tables. They're betting that player ignorance will make such a strategy effective. Don't let them win their bet when it comes to *you*.

You now understand the tactics casino operators use to get you into their establishments, keep you there, and encourage poor play at the tables and slots. You also know the steps you must take to counter these tactics and become a more effective player.

Now what? Can you get into action, confident you've done all you can to make yourself the kind of player casino managers fear the most?

No... because you're only half-way there.

Being a tough player involves more than avoiding the traps and pitfalls casino management has placed in your way. You must do more than just make sure the casino doesn't use you. You've got to go on the offensive and use the casino!

CHAPTER 4

How You Can Use Casinos To Help You Win!

A fledgling gambler once asked me, "How should I choose which casino I play in?"

I thought the answer was obvious until I posed the same question to several other gamblers. Listening to their responses, I discovered that people have many different reasons for choosing a casino, including:

"It's the closest to my home."

"The food is the best I've found anywhere."

"All my friends go there."

"I got the best deal on a four-day gaming package."

"I get golf privileges when I play there."

Hello out there! There's only *one* reason to choose a casino. That's right. Only one. Here it is:

How to Select A Casino

When it comes to choosing a gambling establishment, ask yourself this "bottom-line" question:

"Which casino offers *me* the best chance of winning?"

When you find the answer to that question, you'll know where you should be wagering your money.

If your major reason for gambling is to win, then it only makes sense that you would choose a casino that is compatible with that goal. And here's something else to consider:

The more money you intend to risk in a casino, the more important your casino selection becomes.

Let me illustrate why with an example. Imagine that I make $50,000 a year and I decide to bring a gambling stake of $100 to the casino. Let's assume further that I live in Minnesota and want to play the video poker slots at a casino a few miles from my home. Finally, let's say that I checked the video poker machines in Atlantic City and found out they paid better than the ones near my home. Even though my chances of winning in Atlantic City are better than in Minnesota, the cost of getting to New Jersey—plus the price of meals and a hotel room—

makes the local casino a better overall bet. On the other hand, if I were planning to wager, say, $5,000... then the trip to Atlantic City might well be cost-effective.

In my own experience, I have discovered four factors that are important in determining a casino's "favorableness" for the player.

The first factor centers on *the rules for conducting the various games*. Some casinos play by rules that increase the house's advantage over the player. These are the casinos you'll want to avoid. Other establishments, however, play by rules that are more favorable to the gambler—for example, some may permit 100 times odds at craps or allow doubling down on any two cards in blackjack.

The second factor involves *the payouts on various bets*. Casinos are not obligated to make identical payoffs on various table and slot bets, even when the wagers are the same. And they don't. Some establishments are more "liberal" in the payouts to their customers—returning a higher percentage of the monies wagered. This is true for slot machines, keno, and most table games. In craps, for instance, English casinos give better payouts on certain bets than their American counterparts.

The third factor focuses on *the degree to which the casino hassles winners*. Some establishments are more tolerant of players who consistently beat the house. These casinos are certainly worth locating... and using.

The fourth factor is more difficult to define, but it is definitely a part of every casino. I am referring to *the atmosphere—both physical and psychological—created by the gambling establishment*. This atmosphere is a product of the individual (or corporate) casino owners, and reflects their particular attitudes and policies concerning the way a gaming establishment should be run. This atmosphere, in turn, affects the play of individual gamblers, each with their own attitudes, feelings, and playing peculiarities at the tables. Sometimes the atmosphere increases a gambler's winning potential; other times it hinders chances for success. It all depends on whether the particular casino atmosphere makes players feel comfortable or disturbed at the tables... whether it psychs them out or helps them out.

Because each gambler is unique, there is no one best casino atmosphere for *every* player. An establishment that presents a good winning atmosphere for one individual might have quite the opposite impact on the person standing next to him at the tables.

It becomes imperative, then, that a favorable match be achieved between the unique atmosphere of the individual casino and the unique needs of the individual gambler. The only way *you* can attain such a match is to play in the various casinos and see which ones feel right for you.

Your "Casino Locator" Checklist

Choosing a casino that's right for *you* is a highly personal matter. It involves feelings that are hard to define in scientific terms, attitudes that are difficult to express in words. Nevertheless, by concentrating on the four casino factors I have just presented, you should be in a good position to select those establishments that afford you the best chance of winning.

To make your task easier, I recommend you use a "casino locator checklist" to summarize your impressions of each gaming establishment you visit. A copy of this checklist (filled in with an actual case from my files) is presented later in this chapter). The four items on the checklist correspond to the four factors I have already identified as important in determining a casino's "favorableness" for the player. Note also that there is room for an *"overall ranking/summary"* for the casino you are evaluating. The more casinos you visit the easier it will be to spot differences between them and come up with the overall ranking and summary.

The first letters of the four key terms—Payoffs, Atmosphere, Interaction, and Rules—spell out the word *P.A.I.R.* And it is you and the right casino that create a winning P.A.I.R.

Here are a few suggestions to help you "rate" the various casinos with your checklist:

1. Fill out a separate checklist for *each* game you might play. This is important—as the playing atmosphere and favorability of the different games can vary within the same casino.

2. Complete the checklist as soon as you leave the casino. That way the information will be fresh in your mind and your evaluation will be more accurate.

3. In examining the P.A.I.R. items, ask yourself the following questions:

P = Payoffs: What are the payoffs on the various wagers for the game(s) I intend to play?

Make a mental note on the payoff odds so you can compare them with those offered at other casinos. Once you become familiar with the payoffs at several gaming establishments, it will be relatively easy to pick out gambling "bargains" (payoffs that afford you a greater opportunity for winning). This is because such bargains stand out—just like good prices for a food item at the grocery store. Also, be alert to changes in payoffs over time. As the casino business becomes more competitive, better payoffs are offered as a way to attract customers.

A = Atmosphere: Do I feel comfortable playing in this casino?

Walk around the gaming establishment and get a feeling for its playing atmosphere. Do you feel at ease? Tense? Confident? Insecure? Would you want to play at the tables? Is it too noisy? What about the decor? Is the casino too large or small for you? How do you think you'd do? What you are trying to do is get a feel for the casino's unique atmosphere and see if it fits in with your unique needs. You might not be able to make a final decision without having a go at the tables. If this is the case, go ahead and give it a shot, but play at several establishments before making up your mind on which casino suits you best.

I = Interaction: Is the interaction between players and casino representatives (e.g., dealers, pit bosses) conducive to winning?

Is the interaction friendly and relaxed? Are the dealers courteous and helpful? What about winners—how are they treated? Are they harassed? Would *you* feel comfortable gambling at games supervised and dealt by this casino staff?

R = Rules: What are the rules for the game(s) I intend to play?

Are the rules more favorable for the player than those at other casinos? Remember that rules—like payoffs—can change, so reinvestigate the various gaming establishments at regular intervals. Casinos, like other businesses, can undergo modifications—particularly when there are shakeups in top management. It is possible for a favorable casino to become unfavorable, and vice versa, as the rules, payoffs, employee attitudes, and psychological atmosphere evolve in a particular establishment.

After you have visited several casinos, you will be in a position to compare them, *vis-a-vis* "favorableness" to the player. Once that is accomplished, you'll be able to gamble in those establishments that offer *you* the best chance of winning.

Your Casino Locator Checklist

Date: 3/9/XX
Casino: Lucky's
Game: Craps

P = Payoffs
Standard on pass, come, buy, place. 15-1 on some props.

A = Atmosphere
Ventilation could be better. Tables too large. Low ceilings, too noisy. Only two tables open out of six. Crowded.

I = Interaction
Very friendly crew. Boxman corrected payoff bet in player's favor!

R = Rules
Double odds only. $10.00-$2,000 min/max at table. Call bets not allowed.

Overall Rating/Summary (1 highest; 10 lowest): 5
Good interaction; but rules, atmosphere not favorable.

NOTE: The emphasis in the checklist is on identifying favorable and unfavorable conditions that differentiate various casinos. Note also that judgments on "Atmosphere" and "Interaction" reflect the individual rater's particular needs, and will vary from player to player.

You Gotta Shop Around

If you want to maximize the chances of finding *your* best casino for winning, then, in the words of the old song, "You gotta shop around." As you ponder where to begin, consider this incredible bit of information. It took almost a half-century for legalized casino gambling to spread from Nevada to *one* other location in the United States. Yet, a scant 20 years after Atlantic City opened its first casino, nearly *one-third* of American states was allowing some form of casino gambling within their borders.

This brings us to a good news-bad news scenario. The good news is that casino expansion and competition *will* produce some significant bargains for the player. The bad news is that these bargains will *not* be evenly spread across the U.S.A. In fact, in states and cities where gambling has just been introduced, or only one or two casinos are in operation, players might very well be getting *poor* value for their gambling dollars. Here's the bottom line: The rapid geographical spread of gambling has produced a widening value spread between casinos. Thus, now more than ever before, it is critical to comparison shop to get the most for your wagering dollars.

> As casinos continue to proliferate around the world, it becomes more important than ever to comparison shop if you want to find the casino best suited to your needs and receive top value for the gambling dollars you spend.

Some of you might think that comparison shopping casinos isn't worth the effort. Why is that? Looking for a good casino bargain is no different from looking for good deals on other things you buy. It comes down to this: Would you rather have the money in *your* pocket or somebody else's?

And one thing more: You can realize substantial savings with comparison shopping, particularly on "big ticket" items. Would you forego shopping around when purchasing a car? I doubt it! Well, with what some of you spend gambling per year... we might very well be talking about sums of money that could buy *several* cars!

Finding a casino where you improve your overall winning (or reduce your losing) by just one or two percent can be highly significant when you consider your total betting handle over a trip, a year... or a lifetime. For some gamblers we're talking about differences in the hundreds, thousands—even millions of dollars.

How much did you win or lose last year? How much more could you have won or how much less might you have lost if you had shopped for a casino that gave you the best bargain for your gambling dollars?

Using Las Vegas As A Baseline
For Comparison Shopping

The proliferation of casinos across the United States has left the comparison shopper with a dilemma: "Where do I begin?" So many casinos, so little time! If, for example, you only shop casinos in Minnesota, how do you know if they'll give you a better opportunity to win than, say, the establishments in Mississippi... or any of the other numerous states around the country. Well, one way to find out is to criss-cross the entire country, sampling casinos as you go. Nice idea for a trip, but I suspect a bit too lengthy and costly for most people.

Here's a better idea: Use Las Vegas gaming establishments as a reference for determining the winning potential for any other casino in the country... or the world, for that matter. I make this recommendation because at this time Vegas casinos offer the best gambling bargains and diversity of playing environments in the world.

Here is a gambling destination where you can visit dozens of casinos... all within walking distance of each other. You can compare the Payouts, Atmosphere, Interaction, and Rules in the various establishments and develop a feeling for the kind of casino that gives *you* the greatest chance of winning. Then, when you return to your local gaming venue (whether it be the East, Midwest, or the Gulfport states), you'll know if you're getting the best value for your gambling dollar.

Hey, we've come a long way. You now know the tactics casino operators use against you and what steps you need to take to overcome them. You also know about the importance of casino comparison shopping and how to choose the establishment that's best for *you*. You're ready to sit down at the tables and slots and do some serious winning.

Well... you're not *quite* ready. There's still one more thing you need to do. Something that will strike you as paradoxical when you first think about it. But something that, if done properly, will increase your *enjoyment* and your *winning chances* at the tables. You need to...

Get The Dealer On *Your* Side

What do most gamblers see when they look across the green felt? The enemy. After all, the dealer is hired to protect the casino bankroll—the very thing the player is trying to capture. But does the dealer have to be an enemy? In fact, wouldn't it be better if you could make the dealer an ally rather than an adversary at the tables?

Why should you try to get the dealer on your side?

Let me assure you that establishing a cooperative, rather than a competitive, relationship with a casino dealer is one of the most important things you can do to win—and not get barred from casino action. Yet many players don't understand why this is so.

"Why should I worry about how the dealer feels about me?" many players ask, "especially in games like roulette and craps, where the dealer has no influence over what happens?" The truth of the matter is:

> **Either directly or indirectly, casino dealers can influence whether you win or lose at the tables. That is why it is important to get them on your side as a friend rather than against you as an adversary.**

This is particularly true in blackjack, as we shall soon see, but it also holds true, to varying degrees, throughout the gaming establishment. If a dealer doesn't like you, here are just a few of the things that could happen.

1. A dealer can intimidate you or otherwise make your stay at the tables unpleasant. This tactic, more than any other, can play havoc with a gambler's bankroll and lead to monstrous losses in the casino. Many players, when confronted with a hostile, intimidating casino employee, become unnerved or too aggressive and gamble less effectively. They don't enjoy the gaming experience and they pay dearly for it at the same time. Now that's a double loss in any player's book.

2. Your requests for information or service will be ignored whenever possible. It is amazing how difficult it is to get the attention of a dealer (or order a drink) once that employee wants to ignore you.

3. If you have a complaint against the casino, a dealer can side with the house, making it more difficult for you to win even a legitimate challenge.

4. If you have a dispute with another player (e.g., you and another player both claim the same winning bet on the table), the dealer can side with the other player, making it more likely you will lose the argument.

5. In rare instances you can be "cheated." I put the word in quotes because the cheating of disliked players is a unique kind of dishonesty that can be totally avoided by the gambler who behaves in a civil manner at the tables. Please understand that the vast majority of dealers are honest, hard-working employees doing their best at a trying, often frustrating job.

When they resort to "cheating" a disliked player, it isn't for financial gain or to help the casino. It is used as a last resort to get rid of the customer and to retaliate against treatment they view as grievously inappropriate. Frankly, based on my own observations of obnoxious customers mistreating dealers, I can't say such a payback is entirely inappropriate.

The most common form of this dealer revenge is short-changing the player during payoffs. This can be accomplished much more easily than you might imagine, particularly at the dice table. Most gamblers don't count their payoffs; they just assume the amount is accurate. A chip or two missing every so often is easily overlooked. Think about your own behavior. How often do you check each payoff as it comes from the dealer? In the heat of play, particularly during hot hands where multiple bets and variable payoffs occur at a rapid clip, I know of few gamblers who count their chips each time they are paid. And when a player is excited, tired, or a bit tipsy—which is all too often—the opportunity for successful short-changing is dramatically increased.

Now, then, what happens if a dealer *does* like you? Nice things... like the creation of a playing atmosphere conducive to gambling fun and profit. Here is how dealers can *help* you at the tables:

1. They can increase your profit margin. As in the case of cheating just discussed, this type of dealer help is not usually motivated by the desire for personal profit or to hurt the casino. It is a kind of "thank-you" for your exemplary behavior at the tables. This kind of

dealer activity cannot be carried out with impunity due to casino scrutiny. Thus, it is relatively rare. When it does occur, though, it usually involves over-paying on winning bets or "tipping off" cards (in blackjack).

2. They can ignore call bets or declare them "no bet" when those wagers are losers on the table.

3. They can leave bets on the table even when they lose. This happens most often in craps with the one-roll proposition bets. The dealer "forgets" to take the bet off the layout and it rides for another toss of the dice.

4. A dealer can aid your play by reminding you of certain bets or payoffs you might otherwise have overlooked.

5. In a dispute with the house or another player, the dealer can side with you, making it easier for you to prevail.

6. Your requests for information and service will receive prompt and courteous attention.

7. The dealer will be congenial and help make your gambling more enjoyable. Just as intimidating dealers can unnerve players and reduce their gambling effectiveness, so can friendly dealers psychologically support players and enhance their level of play at the tables.

As an added point of interest: There have been claims that some blackjack dealers can manipulate the order of cards dealt (even from a shoe) to either help or hurt a player. Further, rumors persist about roulette dealers skillful enough to steer the ball toward or away from a specific part of the wheel. If either of these rumors are true, I wouldn't want my blackjack or roulette dealer mad at me! Would you?

It is always to your advantage to get the dealer on your side when it comes to gambling in a casino. In the case of blackjack, it is absolutely essential, particularly if you count cards. In 21, if a dealer doesn't like you, he can shut you down, pure and simple. And he doesn't have to cheat to do it, either. All he has to do is tell the pit boss he suspects you of counting. Sorrowful times will surely follow.

On the other hand, if a blackjack dealer likes you, he can increase your profit potential by helping you with your hit or stand decisions. If the dealer knows his downcard does not make his hand pat (a small card instead of 10-value card, for example), he might pass by your spot on the table instead of stopping for your decision. Call it an unsolicited signal... friend to friend.

I've even seen cases where a dealer will shuffle early, shuffling away a 10-poor deck. And who hasn't seen a player get a privileged peak at the burn-cards or the dealer's down-card? It happens. But this is certainly not to say that it's prevalent.

Regardless, there is no other casino game where the dealer can have such an influence in terms of cold, hard cash.

The next time you sit down at a blackjack table and eye the dealer across the green felt, keep his or her importance in mind. That's one person you want on your side, rooting *for* you rather than against you.

How Can I Get The Dealer On My Side?

Good question, glad you asked. Civility helps. Understanding the dealer does, too.

A dealer's job isn't all gravy. Understanding the hassles casino employees face will help you interact with them more effectively. For example, dealers in some casinos are under pressure by management to make sure the house wins (particularly in blackjack, where the house knows the game can be beaten). The dealers aren't expected to cheat for the house, but if they seem to lose consistently, the pit bosses aren't exactly overjoyed.

To make matters worse, most gamblers expect to win, too. And they put pressure on the dealers when they don't. This leaves dealers between a rock and a hard place. If they win too often they're hassled by irate players, and if they don't win often enough they're criticized by casino management.

Put yourself in the dealer's place. How would *you* like to work under such circumstances? Throw in long workdays and lack of employment security, and you have one hell of a job! I'd venture to say that if the average gambler were suddenly thrust into the role of dealer, he or she would come away from the experience with a healthy respect for the men and women behind the tables.

Which brings us back to your question: How *can* you get the dealers on your side? The answer is to treat them

the way you'd want to be treated. Remember, casino dealers are no different from other human beings. They need,
they ache, they love, they hate—just as you and I do. If
you treat them with kindness, they will respond accordingly. The problem is—as I mentioned earlier—most players don't see the dealer as someone who deserves such
treatment. They see the dealer as the enemy, someone to
beat.

The problem with viewing the dealers as the enemy is
that you treat them like enemies. This, in turn, causes the
dealer to treat you in a similar fashion. It is a vicious
circle, and an unpleasant one, for the dealer and player
alike.

A Partnership, Not A War

What I am going to ask you to do is make a *paradigm
shift*. I want you to see the dealer as an ally, not a foe. I
want you to establish a partnership, not a contest, between you and the dealer. If you can't stop thinking of
the dealer as an enemy, then go ahead and think it. But
don't *treat the dealer as an enemy*. Instead, behave in the
following manner at the tables:

1. Be friendly and courteous to casino personnel. Most
    dealers are accustomed to abuse and rude behavior
    from players who see them as the enemy. Thus, they
    appreciate gamblers who treat them with kindness
    and respect.

2. Don't act as though you are better than the dealer.
    This is not an ego contest you're involved in. It is an
    activity where you are trying to win some money.

3. When you are winning, "toke" (tip) the dealer. Think
    of the tip as an investment in dealer goodwill. This is
    particularly important in blackjack, for reasons I've
    already discussed. It is not necessary to *overtip* in
    order to gain dealer goodwill. You should tip in pro-
    portion to your bet size and winnings—not to im-
    press the dealer or to give away your hard-earned
    profits in outlandish tokes. Remember, you're buck-
    ing some pretty rough percentages when you sit down
    at the tables. The dealers realize this and don't ex-
    pect you to give them a big chunk of everything you
    win.

    When you do tip, make it in the form of a bet for
    the dealer. For instance, in craps, if you're betting
    the pass-line, make a pass-line wager "for the deal-
    ers." In blackjack, when you make a wager, occa-
    sionally make one for the dealer, too, *before* the cards
    are dealt. That way if you win, so does the dealer.
    This kind of tipping will help underscore your part-
    ner relationship with the dealer, the idea that you
    both need each other for a winning session.

4. Don't be afraid to play against a dealer of the oppo-
    site sex. When you do, be friendly and cheerful. It
    helps brighten up a dealer's otherwise dull routine.
    Some players feel that a bit of tasteful flirtation can
    sometimes work wonders for making a dealer more
    responsive to the gambler's needs as a player *and* a

person. In some cases they might be right, but as a general rule I'd recommend *against* using such a strategy. In this day and age, unwanted flirtations can lead to much unpleasantness and gnashing of teeth. It's not worth it.

5. Strike up a conversation with the dealer if you can do so comfortably and will not be distracted from play. Not all dealers like to speak with customers but many appreciate the opportunity to move beyond the mechanical level of player/dealer interaction.

6. When dealers do a good job at the tables, it never hurts to praise them for their efforts. I make it a point to compliment dealers whenever I feel they have provided me with good service. I think they deserve the praise—and it makes them feel better about me *and* their job.

7. When you establish good rapport with certain dealers, be sure to remember who they are. That way you will be able to identify and target them for additional play in the future.

8. Not everybody is going to like you, no matter how hard you try. If you're playing against a dealer who remains hostile despite your best efforts, move to another table. Or, if the option exists, move to another casino. There are many dealers out there in casinoland. Don't get stuck with one who wants to see you lose.

In summary, the next time you sit down to play in the casino, view the dealer across the table as your friend, not your foe... as your partner, not your adversary. Be congenial and treat that person with respect. If you do, you'll feel better as a person and do better as a player at the same time.

Before I end this chapter I'd like to examine one last procedure for using casinos effectively. Hopefully, you won't have cause to use the information very often, but if the time comes when you must... well, it might end up saving you some significant bucks.

Disputing Casino Decisions

It happened at a dice table in Atlantic City. It was my turn to shoot. Standing in my favorite position, to the immediate right of the stickman, I picked up two "lucky" dice and sent them tumbling down the table. "Nine, nine in the field, nine," intoned the stickman, deftly retrieving the dice and nudging them in my direction.

I scooped up the two translucent cubes and tossed them again, shouting "niner on the liner" for encouragement. One die came to rest quite normally, flat on the table, the number 5 face up. Not so for the second die, which ricocheted about, finally coming to rest in a "tilt" position, leaning against a pile of chips at a crazy angle. I gave a shout and victory salute, as the number 4 seemed uppermost from my vantage point.

Then it happened. "Seven, pay the don'ts," announced the stickman. From across the table a dealer began reaching for my pass-line bet.

"Wait a minute," I blurted, my voice a mixture of shock and disbelief. "I just made my point!"

"Sorry," replied the boxman, joining the discussion. "Five and two is seven in my book."

"Five and *two?*" My voice edged higher. "Where do you see a two?"

"Here," the dealer broke in, pointing with the curved edge of his stick at one face of the die with two pips on it. It was then I realized that, depending on the person's viewing angle, an argument could be made for different sides of the cube being the "correct" number.

While I stood silently, considering my response to the dilemma, the stickman swept the tilted die from its precarious resting place and, with it, any claim that I might have made.

I was furious but there was nothing I could do. I doubled my line bet to "get back" what was rightfully mine. This, of course, was a dumb thing to do. One should never double up after a loss, as we will see in the next chapter. But, I thought, justice was on my side. Well, justice might have been, but luck wasn't! I lost that bet and got all the madder... and all the dumber. I doubled up again. And lost. I won't even describe the brutal end to this little incident, except to say that when dice go on tilt, humans often follow.

From Disaster Comes Wisdom

Even a mistake can be turned to your long-term advantage if you learn from it. And when it comes to using— rather than being used by—casinos, sometimes a mistake can teach you the right way to approach the tables at a later date. Such was the case with the "tilted die." What it taught me was this:

> Always dispute any casino decision you don't agree with.

Many players won't do this. They are too shy, or too insecure, or embarrassed. Or (just like me) a bit stupid. Whatever the reason, it doesn't justify your silence. Dealers aren't gods. They make mistakes like everybody else. The problem is, these dealer mistakes can cost you *money*. Therefore, don't be afraid to speak up if you have a question, challenge, or an objection. And do so *quickly*—before the situation changes through continued play.

Actually it is financially irresponsible not to challenge any playing decision you disagree with. This is because many casinos have a "customer is right the first time" policy. What this means, in practice, is that the casino will allow your claim the first time you dispute a payoff or some other dealer action. Don't expect such cooperative behavior the second time around, however!

Recommended Steps To Follow In Challenging A Casino Decision

If you believe a casino employee has made a mistake such as an incorrect payoff on your bet, misinterpretation of your hand, wrong placement of your wager, or giving another player your payoff during a gambling session:

1. **Take immediate action.** This is critical, as hesitation in making your claim can result in destruction of the evidence, such as a stickman removing a tilted die from its precarious perch.

2. **Try to minimize alterations of the "playing environment."** This holds true even *before* a claim is made. Let me give you an example. Let us assume you've just hit a winner at the dice table and the dealer has just completed paying off your bet. Now what do you do? Many players immediately pick up the chips and count them in their hands. Others don't count them until they place the chips in the rail in front of them. Either of these two actions involve major alterations of the playing environment and lessen the chances of getting additional chips, even if the payout was wrong. My suggestion is that you *always* check your payouts while the chips are still on the table (this is easy to do in any game other than craps where you don't want to get in the way of the dice). That way if there is a dispute, all the evidence is right where it was left, by the dealer and you.

3. **Be polite.** Don't bellow or scream out about "casino injustice." Even if a casino employee *did* make a mistake, it doesn't mean it was made on purpose. Overwhelming odds are it was an accident, the kind anyone could make, even you and I. If you get nasty with casino staff you reduce your chances of gaining management sympathy and concurrence with your point of view.

4. **State your case clearly and calmly.** Flustered play-
    ers often muddle up their claims, thereby lessening
    the likelihood for a favorable casino response.

5. **Be prepared to "appeal" any adverse decision if
    you feel your claim has not been appropriately
    resolved.** If the casino floorperson at your table does
    not agree with your point of view and you wish to
    press the issue further, ask to see the floor supervi-
    sor or shift boss. In cases where physical evidence is
    important to your claim, request that the game be
    stopped until your case is settled. (Sometimes a re-
    quest to delay the game until a supervisor can be
    found will trigger the table staff to go ahead and pay
    your claim on the spot. *Nobody* likes a game to be
    halted, particularly the casino operators who know
    the casino makes money only when the cards and
    dice keep moving.)

    If management refuses to stop the game or your
    appeal is rejected by the floor supervisor, don't make
    a scene. You still have the option of carrying your
    challenge to higher levels; for example, the casino
    manager or the casino regulatory agency that has
    jurisdiction over the casino where your dispute took
    place.

6. **In situations where the physical evidence support-
    ing your claim is no longer available (in my case
    when the dealer removed the tilted die from its
    position on the table) you have the option of re-
    questing casino surveillance tapes that might con-
    tain video footage of your dispute.**

7. **Whether you win or lose your claim, stop playing
   at once if you feel flustered, angry, or distracted
   by the chain of events.** Frankly, I would recommend that a player *always* take a forced "leave of
   action" from the tables *whenever* a casino action
   seems unjustified. Why play on when you feel you
   have been poorly treated? It can't be much fun for
   you. Besides, such a belief normally leads to
   "revenge" play with all its undesirable side effects
   (carelessness, "steaming" disrupted concentration,
   etc.).

Challenging a casino decision should never be under-
taken without good reason. Yet, done properly—with
politeness, immediacy, and clarity—it can help educate
casino personnel and bring you "justice" at the same time.
That's a player edge worth fighting for.

The Green Felt Schism

In my three decades of casino gambling, I have noted
one disturbing trend: a growing rift between casino management and casino gamblers. Casino owners and players
have not always been at odds. In competition, yes, but
not at each other's throats. In fact, when I first began
playing in Las Vegas there was a great deal of camaraderie across the tables.

Dealers were, in large part, friendly and cheerful. So
were the pit bosses. Gamblers still lost more than they
won, but the ambiance and goodwill generated by casino
personnel seemed to take the sting out of the house percentage.

Then things began to change. Corporations took over many major gaming establishments. The casinos were staffed with executives who knew very little about gamblers' needs or peculiarities. At the same time, cost-cutting accountants dulled the power of the pencil and took issue with the personalized credit policies extended to players.

Casinos took on a more "business-like" appearance, with the gambler becoming more of a customer and less of a personal friend. Rising costs of running a casino didn't help either. It put casino owners in a cost squeeze and forced them to cut out (or charge more for) many services that kept gamblers happy.

Then came the most serious blow to casino-gambler relations: the discovery and subsequent widespread utilization of card-counting techniques at blackjack. With it came a whole era of distrust, recrimination, and hostility that festered like a disease at the 21 tables. It spread throughout the casino, infecting players, dealers, pit bosses, and casino executives alike. It was a full-blown epidemic of paranoia across the green felt.

Every time a player won at blackjack, the pit boss wondered if a professional counter was out to drain the casino coffers. Every time a player lost, he wondered if he was being cheated—after all, the game *was* supposed to be beatable. Meanwhile, the poor dealer, caught in the middle of this tug of war, wasn't in very good spirits either.

To make matters worse, reports began circulating that several counters had been mistreated, manhandled, cheated, and barred from the casinos. For many players, particularly the regular, higher-limit gamblers, this information was particularly disturbing. And not just for those playing blackjack. Crapshooters, roulette players, and baccarat enthusiasts all began to wonder: "If 21 players could be treated in such a manner, what's to stop the casino from pulling a fast one on *me?*"

It was a disturbing question, and the casinos did little to provide a satisfactory answer. They, too, felt threatened and were not at all happy about being perceived as the "enemy." In many cases they responded defensively and angrily to players' charges. A calmer, more considered reaction would have been the wiser choice.

As tempers flared, the bond of mutual trust and respect—so vital to the harmonious balance between gambler and casino personnel—frayed and snapped. For many, the era of the green felt schism had begun.

A Silver Lining

All this distrust and paranoia has produced one positive benefit: Many regular players have become more suspicious and less satisfied in the new casino atmosphere. They have not been as easily "psyched" out by the casino "hype" and have become more careful, rational gamblers. This is great.

Yet if the current gulf between gambler and casino continues to widen, the very survival of casino gaming might be at stake. After all, gamblers are the very lifeblood of any casino. When they stop flowing through the front doors, the establishment dies. And in today's economy, where scant profit margins allow little room for error, that death can come quickly—and almost without warning.

Does the possible demise of casino gambling make me happy? No. I'm a casino gambler and I need gaming establishments if I want to continue playing. Rooting for the demise of casinos would be like an astronaut cheering for an end to the space program. Therefore, I'm going to recommend that casinos and players forge a new relationship in the 21st century. Before I describe what that relationship should be, let me tell you a story:

A Story With A Moral

This story is about *Adamsia palliata* and *Pagurus prideauxi*. No, they aren't Latin quarter horses, although they are excellent "mudders" and can move swiftly through water. In fact, *Adamsia palliata* is a strawberry cloaklet sea anemone, and *Pagurus prideauxi* is a type of hermit crab.

These little underwater creatures share a very interesting and mutually beneficial life together. The anemone wraps itself around the shell in which the hermit crab is living. By positioning its mouth and tentacles beneath the mouth of *Pagurus prideauxi*, it is able to share the food taken by its host.

What does the hermit crab get in exchange for sharing its meal? Protection, for one thing. It turns out that *Adamsia palliata* is no slouch when it comes to playing the "heavy" and it keeps unwanted predators away. In addition, the anemone is a home builder. It can enlarge the crab's domicile by secreting an extension to the shell. This makes it unnecessary for *Pagurus prideauxi* to change shells as it grows.

Adamsia palliata and *Pagurus prideauxi* are very dependent on each other for survival. In fact, should the hermit crab decide to leave home, the anemone will perish unless it can find another host.

This brings us to the moral of this little tale: Survival sometimes depends on the development of a *symbiotic relationship*. This is defined as "the intimate living together of two dissimilar organisms in a mutually beneficial relationship."

Achieving A Balanced Symbiotic Relationship Between The Gambler And The Casino

Due to several problems already discussed, casino management and some casino gamblers have come to see each other as natural enemies. Such a belief, narrowly conceived, is understandable, considering that both parties *are* in competition across the tables.

Yet, in broader perspective, nothing could be further from the truth! In reality, gamblers and casino owners are *not* enemies. Like *Adamsia palliata* and *Pagurus prideauxi*, they share a symbiotic relationship: Neither can survive without the other.

Casino owners and casino gamblers are like Siamese twins, joined together in a mutual struggle for survival. You can't cut off one half and expect the other half to survive and prosper. What would happen, for instance, if all gamblers quit playing or kept winning *all* the time? How long do you think the casinos would stay open?

Conversely, what would be the outcome if casino personnel barred all gamblers from the premises or beat them out of every penny they had? How long do you think the doors would stay open then?

If gambling is to survive in the 21st century, we'll need to establish a *balanced symbiotic relationship* between casino gamblers and casino management. Both parties to this relationship must recognize they need each other to survive.

Further, they must understand that this survival depends on the establishment and maintenance of a *power balance* between the player and the gaming establishment. If one party becomes too powerful, it can destroy the other party completely. That's about as reasonable as biting the hand that feeds you.

Instituting an effective symbiotic relationship will necessitate some extensive fence-mending on both sides of the green felt. It will also require gamblers and casino management alike to develop new ideas and procedures for use in gaming establishments. For instance, casino management should be allowed to create games and gaming environments that help them beat the player, but they should not employ tactics like the "stretch and break" that encourage players to gamble beyond their means.

Again, the whole purpose of restraint on both sides of the table is to maintain a *balanced* symbiotic relationship. Such a relationship is vital to the well-being of casino gamblers and management alike.

Once casino management and players accept a reconciliation as necessary for mutual survival, and come to believe in a symbiotic rather than adversarial model for interpersonal relations, a new era of cooperation and good feeling can commence.

Please don't get me wrong. I am *not* saying that it is unhealthy or unnatural to allow a "competitive" position between gambler and casino. Competition and differences of opinion can be healthy to all parties, if carried out in the proper spirit and context. But it should be constructive rather than destructive competition.

Casino gambling provides a natural opportunity for achieving a balanced symbiotic relationship between casino player and casino management. It is my hope that such a relationship can be established and maintained in the years to come, paving the way for a healthier, more satisfying gaming experience on both sides of the table.

SECTION THREE

The Three Levels Of Gambling Stupidity That Cost You Money: Dumb, Dumber, And Dumbest

> Knowledge and human power are synonymous.
>
> *Francis Bacon*

CHAPTER 5

Domain Of The Dumb

This chapter could have been titled "Look Ma, No Brains" or "Dumbing Down in Casino Town." It's about players who do some really stupid things, players like me (I told you I learned the hard way) and, I suspect, players like you, too. Hey, the real problem with playing stupid isn't doing it... it's continuing to do it once you know better.

Let me ask you a question. Suppose you want to buy some stocks. One broker charges over 5 percent to handle your transaction, while another will do it for under 3 percent. There is no difference in level of service between the two brokers. Which broker would you use?

Here's a second question. Let's say you have money to risk, and you're considering two similar investments. One investment, however, could be made at half the risk of the other. Which investment would you choose?

"Such simple questions," you say, "with such obvious answers." So tell me, how do you explain this: In certain Nevada casinos you can play roulette on either an "American" or "European" wheel. The house advantage on the American wheel is almost double that of the European model (5.26 percent vs. 2.70 percent), yet the American wheels attract players—even when the "better deal" European models are just a few steps away on the casino floor.

Playing an American wheel when a European model is available, is equivalent to using the 5 percent broker, or choosing the investment that was double the risk.

Gambling authority Allan Wilson is puzzled by this seemingly senseless behavior. "It will forever be a mystery to [me] why roulette players did not *flock* to the clubs that first introduced the more generous [European] wheel. An even bigger mystery is how these clubs that sport *both* types of wheels can do any business on the two-zero [American] wheel."

Allan Wilson is being kind. In fact, there is no mystery to this behavior at all. The simple, sad truth is that when it comes to gambling, many players check their brains at the casino door.

My own casino observations have convinced me that many casino players are bent on attaining the lowest common denominator of human intelligence at the tables. Some players just don't know anything about the games. They blindly place their bets, hoping that some divine force will intercede on their behalf. Others *seem* to know what they're doing, but what they're doing is *incredibly* stupid... which makes matters all the worse. In some ways their actions might almost be humorous if they weren't so pitiful. And costly.

Ignorance Isn't Bliss

Let me share with you just a few examples of "brain-less" gambling I have had the misfortune of witnessing during my casino visits. These are *not* isolated cases. If I told you of all the inept play I've observed at the tables and slots, neither of us would ever finish this book.

ITEM: I was watching a player at the blackjack tables. He was dealt two aces. "I'm busted," he said, flipping his cards over for the dealer to see.

"What do you mean?" the dealer inquired, not know-ing quite what to make of the situation.

"I got a twenty-two... isn't that a bust?"

The dealer was flabbergasted. So was I. And I'll bet you thought splitting tens was a dumb move. I didn't wait around to see the rest of the carnage.

ITEM: Another intellectual giant was perched at the rail of the craps table betting $5 chips on the BIG 6 and BIG 8. I asked him why he didn't *place* the 6 and 8, and get better odds at 7 to 6.

"What's a *place* bet?" the player wanted to know. I realized he'd have to find out in a hurry. With the extra house edge he was bucking by betting BIG 6 and BIG 8... he wouldn't be around for very long.

ITEM: Walking through the casino after lunch one day, I spotted a woman playing roulette. She was betting the "Martingale" progression, chasing her money with a ven-geance. I sidled up and asked how she was doing.

"I've won $50 already," she replied proudly.

"You're doubling up after a loss, right?"

"Yes, how did you know?" (It's amazing how many people think their "system" is a gambling secret known only to a few.)

"I played it myself once. You know," I added, "if you hit a run of bad luck it could wipe you out real quick."

The lady looked at me like *I* was crazy. "My brother-in-law has been using this method for years... and it's paid for all his trips to the casino."

What could I say? I hate in-laws who lie.

ITEM: I was heading past the casino on my way to my car when I spotted a woman playing the progressive video slots. She was at a bank of quarter machines sporting a very juicy $2,700+ jackpot. I watched her for a few moments, noticing that she was playing only one quarter at a time... never the 5-coin maximum needed to win the progressive jackpot. You guessed it: The inevitable happened and *she hit a royal flush!* A shower of coins spilled into the payout-bowl, much to her delight.

It was then that the man next to her ruined everything. "Too bad," he said to the smiling woman.

The woman turned to him, perplexed. "What do you mean?" she said curiously, her graphite-black fingers scooping the newly dispensed coins into a nearby cup.

"You could've gotten a much bigger payout," he explained.

"Bigger than *this?*" The woman shook her cupful of coins.

"Much bigger. Over *two thousand dollars bigger!*"

The woman's eyes opened real wide. "*What* $2,000 are you talking about?"

"There…" The man pointed to the jackpot figure above the bank of machines. "You needed to put in five quarters to get it."

"I didn't know…" The woman's voice trailed off in a gasp. "I mean to say, nobody told me I could win *that* much money."

I wanted to tell her: "Well, if that doesn't take the jackpot." But I didn't. Honest.

Would you like to know the really sad thing about the woman losing her jackpot? She's not an isolated case. Every year a king's ransom in jackpot dollars goes unpaid because players didn't take the time to learn about the payouts on their machines.

When it comes to casino gambling, the odds are tough enough to beat in the first place. To give the house an extra edge through ignorance or stupidity is literally presenting it with a license to steal.

> Gamble smart… or don't gamble at all. Learn the game(s) you intend to play *before* you risk your money playing them. A "no brainer" might be a winning hand in Gin Rummy, but it's a loser at the tables. Play intelligently and you'll be playing to win.

Ignorance Is Costly

In previous years, ignorance at the tables often led to financial loss—the players made mistakes that cost them

money. Yet in one way these gamblers were fortunate:
There wasn't much variation in casino rules or games.
Knowing, for example, that a two-zero roulette wheel
was a poorer bet than a one-zero model didn't matter
much because virtually every American casino used two-
zero wheels exclusively.

Ahh, but how times have changed! With the proliferation of gambling establishments, some casinos have been
forced into "price wars"... wars that provide significant
bargains for the *knowledgeable* bettor. What kind of bargains? Basically, in the amount of house advantage a casino is willing to be satisfied with.

It is instructive to note the degree to which this gaming
expansion has forced casinos to offer customers better
percentage games. A good example is provided by the
"odds-bet" on the craps table.

In the 1970s when I first began gambling in Las Vegas,
it was basically a "single odds" town. As the number of
Nevada gambling establishments increased, a few casinos
(primarily downtown) began dealing "double odds." Still,
double-odds games were the exception, particularly on
the Strip. Then came the '80s and '90s with the rapid
expansion of casinos in Nevada and throughout the country.

The scramble for customers was on!

The result? Establishments began offering double odds
as a matter of course, while some casinos made the ultimate offer a crapshooter couldn't refuse: **100 times odds!**
(I personally flew to Mississippi the first time *that* offer
was made at Binion's Horseshoe in Tunica. A wild and
woolly time was had by all.) Similar types of player-
favorable changes in gaming rules such as a lower rake

percentage in poker games, 4 percent commission on banker hands in baccarat, single zero rules in roulette, for example, are sweeping the casino industry. These changes are offering *knowledgeable* gamblers a better chance of winning. I hope you're one of them.

Gamble Tough

Knowledge *is* power in the world of casino gaming. Here are three rules to help you gain that power through intelligent play.

1. **Play only those games you fully understand.** Would you invest your hard-earned money in a business you didn't understand? I suspect not. So why behave differently at the tables?

2. **Restrict your action to casinos with the most favorable rules and payoffs.** Keep in mind that casino and airline bargains are similar: They are constantly changing and must be regularly monitored to get the best deals.

3. **Keep away from wagers where the house advantage exceeds 1.6 percent.** As I indicated in Chapter 2, I would prefer that you restrict your play to *positive expectation* casino activities; but if you must wager on *negative expectation* games, at least you give yourself a gambling chance for short-term wins when you restrict your action to the low-house-edge wagers.

Follow these three rules and you'll be a tough player, the kind of player that casino managers fear the most. What gambler can ask for more?

I can, and so can you, because **playing smart helps you in a second crucial way. It makes you feel more competent, confident, clear-headed, and capable of self-control.** These are feelings that not only help you play more effectively at the tables; they also immunize you against many of the casino tactics used to encourage poor gambling.

An Effort-Saving Suggestion

Gambling smart will get you the most for your gaming dollar. If you don't intend to gamble intelligently, take my advice. Decide how much money you intend to take on your next gambling trip, write that amount on a check, and mail it to the casino you were planning to visit. That way you can save the time and cost of actually *going* to the casino and still give yourself about the same chance of winning as if you had actually played at the tables.

CHAPTER 6

Domicile Of The Dumber

Here are two exact opposite wagering systems that are used in the casino. Which one comes closest to the way you bet?

Strategy # 1:

You maintain or reduce your betting level when you are losing.

Strategy # 2:

You increase your bet(s) when you are losing in an attempt to recoup your money.

If you answered "Strategy #1"... congratulations, you are a tough player who *"doesn't chase your losses"* in the casino.

If you answered "Strategy #2"... welcome to the Domicile of the Dumber.

Hey, you're not alone, you know! The great majority of gamblers are Strategy #2 devotees... which is one reason why casinos win billions of dollars from their customers every year.

And here's a personal admission to make you feel better: I—your humble author—have spent a good portion of my gambling life inhabiting the Domicile of the Dumber. I admit it. I know it's wrong. And most of the money I have lost at the tables and slots has been the direct result of this stupid, dumber-than-dumb behavior.

Oh, how many times I have played through this scenario. I'm at the tables betting in a reasonable, measured fashion. Suddenly, I lose three or four bets in a row. Now I "throw good money after bad," increasing the size of my bets in an attempt to get my lost money back... *fast*. The losing streak continues. I pump in bigger and bigger bets, assuming the tide *has* to turn. It doesn't turn. I'm washed out... wiped out... kaput... *Hasta la vista, Baby*.

A Recent Tragedy In One Act

Let me give you a recent example of my own *domicile of the dumber* folly. I do so not to encourage you to emulate my foolish action but, rather, to warn you how easy it is to fall victim to such behavior.

When I first began this project, I researched various topics and tested various wagering strategies for the book. One test involved taking all the money I had left (at the time the test was conducted) and seeing if I could wager it in a controlled fashion when the safeguards I used to regulate my betting were missing. Thus, instead of bringing just a portion of my bankroll to the table—and keeping the remaining amount safely tucked away in a distant lockbox—I took the entire bankroll with me.

As I have already pointed out, keeping a portion of your bankroll out of easy reach is a good way to reduce the risk of chasing your losses, should the cards or dice turn against you. The reason? Because you have to *leave* the gambling area to get more ammunition. Getting away from the table, along with the time it takes you to retrieve extra gambling funds, is often all that's needed to "cool you down" and stop your headlong rush to financial oblivion.

It works kind of like the dieting procedure where a diner is required to leave the table immediately after dinner and not allowed to consume desert until at least ten minutes have passed. Many individuals who observe this restriction discover that their desire for dessert dissipates a few minutes after leaving the table and they can pass it up altogether.

It appears that the hunger for unhealthy eating *and* betting can be reduced by placing a required "time out" during action at the table.

At any rate, I thought I would be strong enough to control my own wagering without the protection afforded me by limiting my readily available cash reserves.

I thought wrong!

Even after decades of gambling I still was susceptible to "throwing good money after bad"—chasing my losses until I had nothing left to lose. Less than one hour later,

I realized that not using the safeguards I recommend in this book was a bad mistake.

A *big* mistake.

Don't you make the same mistake.

I can assure you I won't... ever again!

What about *you*? Could my story be *your* story?

Be honest with yourself!

For you players who *do* bet more when you're losing, I have a suggestion. The next time you find yourself losing and betting bigger to "get back in the game," recall the following statement. Maybe it will help you keep your betting in check. It has worked for me.

There are losing streaks and there are winning streaks. If you are in a losing pattern, learn to ride it out, pull in your horns, and conserve your bankroll. Wait patiently for the tide to turn. That way, if it does, you'll still be around to take advantage of it.

> **Chasing your losses by making bigger bets when you are losing is a *very* bad idea. Never do it. Learning to control yourself when you're in the middle of a losing streak can be a *very* trying experience... but it's a great character builder. If you can maintain your mental resolve in the crucible of a losing crisis and not "steam" your way into oblivion, you will be a stronger, wiser, and richer person for it.**

CHAPTER 7

Dominion Of The Dumbest

Here's a well-traveled gambling joke for you. A man named Fred pays an unexpected visit to his friend, Steve.

"Steve, you've *gotta* help me," Fred pleads. "I'm not getting paid till next week and I don't have any money to buy groceries or get my wife to the doctor." He pauses for effect. "My wife *really* needs to see the doctor, Steve."

"How much are we talking about?" Steve asks warily.

"Not that much," Fred assures his friend. "Five hundred dollars should do it."

"I don't know..." Steve says, his voice trailing off.

"I'll pay you back in a week... I promise."

Steve remains silent.

"*Please,* Steve," Fred pleads, sensing his friend is wavering between yes and no.

"All right, then," Steve decides. He gets $500 from a cash box in his bedroom and hands it to Fred. As Fred opens his billfold to put the money away, Steve notices some hundred-dollar bills sticking out.

"What's that?!" he exclaims, pointing at the wallet. "I thought you said you didn't have any money to pay for food or your wife's doctor."

"I don't," Fred responds.

Steve stares at his friend in disbelief. "Well, then, what about those Franklins in your wallet?"

"Oh that. That's *gambling* money."

Fred has just become a charter member of the *Dominion of the Dumbest*. He has earned this dubious honor by doing the stupidest thing a gambler can do. He has violated the most basic rule in gambling:

> **Never gamble more than you can *comfortably* afford to lose. Whenever you risk amounts of money that, if lost, would force changes in your lifestyle, you are wagering too much.**

Please, *please* don't enter this dominion. If you're already there, get out as fast as you can. Gambling more than you can comfortably afford to lose creates all kinds of problems, including:

1. **A greater likelihood that you will lose your bankroll.** If you gamble more than you can comfortably afford to lose, there is a good chance it will affect your judgment during play. You are wagering what is known as "scared money" and professional gamblers will tell you that "scared money invariably loses."

2. **A greater likelihood that you will become an addicted gambler.** When people first start gambling more than they can comfortably afford to lose, they start down the slippery slope to gambling degeneracy. If they don't get hold of themselves and claw their way up from the abyss, they will end up gambling away everything... *period*.

3. **A greater likelihood that your personal life—and the lives of those around you—will suffer.** The price of gambling more than you can comfortably afford to lose is a likely deterioration in your quality of life and the fallout that invariably accompanies it: shattered hopes, careers, and relationships.

Considering the bad things that can happen when players gamble more than they can afford to lose, you might wonder who would ever be foolish enough to gamble that way in the first place.

I did. Like many others who get caught up in the feverpitch of gambling excitement, I wasn't really aware of how serious my gambling problem had become. Gamblers are great rationalizers and self-deceivers. They are a lot like the woman who, confronted by the signs of her husband's infidelity (lipstick on shirt, perfume scent on jacket, unusual pattern of late nights at "work"), mentally refuses to see the evidence before her. She doesn't *want* to see it. So, too, the gambler ignores or rationalizes away the signs of his degenerate affair with Lady Luck: the unpaid bills, the mounting debt, the cash advances on the credit cards.

How about you? Are you certain *your* gambling hasn't put you in the Domicile of the Dumbest? Have you paused lately to consider what impact *your* gambling is having on your financial health? Can you confidently say you are not wagering more than you can afford to lose? These are questions you need to answer... preferably, *before* your next visit to a casino. Now, here's a final question I'd like you to answer right away.

How much money must you wager to keep casino action exciting?

Please make an attempt to arrive at a figure that accurately and honestly answers the question from *your* point of view. A true, carefully considered response is vital because it can be used to help you determine whether or not gambling *has* become dangerous to your psychological and financial health. So please... take some time with this question before reading on.

Now then—a little psychology. Regardless of what figure(s) you came up with in answering the question, there are three basic principles that help explain the relationship between wagering levels and gambling excitement.

1. There are individual differences in the amount of money people need to bet to keep casino action exciting. That is, one person might be "on the edge of his seat" betting $5 chips at the craps table, while another gambler might require a $2,000 wager on every baccarat decision to keep things "interesting."

2.   Generally, the wealthier a person is, the higher the wager must be to keep gaming exciting. For example, a person who makes $100,000 a year would likely find a $25 bet less exciting than the individual who brings home $25,000 annually.

3.   The longer or more frequently a person gambles, the higher the likelihood that he will have to wager increasing amounts of money to keep casino action at an acceptable level of excitement. In actual casino terms, what this means is that over time, the nickel slot player will want to "graduate" to the dime, quarter, and eventually $1 slots. Similarly, the $1 bettor at the blackjack table will, over time, want to raise his betting stakes to $5, $10, and even more.

This phenomenon is not unique to the casino gambler. In fact, almost any activity, carried out over time, has the tendency to become less exciting unless steps are taken to maintain or increase interest in the undertaking. In jogging, that might mean running faster or farther the longer a person participates in the activity. In gambling it often means betting bigger or faster when wagering at the tables.

When it comes to casino wagering, it is almost as if the gambler—like a person taking a prescribed narcotic—becomes "adapted" to a certain level of betting "dosage" over time, and must increase the potency of his wager if he wants to experience the same level of excitement as he has in the past.

An interesting experiment was conducted along these lines. A mobile with two rattles was placed over a baby's crib. After the baby had played with the toy for a while, the mobile was replaced with a new one that had three rattles. Again the baby was allowed to play with it. Twice more the mobile was replaced, once with a four-rattle model and, finally, one with five rattles. The baby played enthusiastically with each new mobile as it was placed over its crib. However, when the mobile with five rattles was replaced with the original mobile containing only two rattles, the baby wanted nothing to do with it! The moral: Once you're used to playing with five rattles, two rattles just doesn't cut it anymore. And once you're used to betting black ($100) chips, returning to the days of betting red ($5) chips often doesn't cut it, either.

What Price Excitement?

For the *sensible* gamblers, the price of excitement at the casino will *never* be too high. That is, they will be able to keep gambling interesting while wagering safe amounts of money. They have learned, purposely or intuitively, never to bet more than they can comfortably afford to lose.

These individuals have a sensible attitude toward casino wagering. They are willing to risk money to take a shot at both excitement *and* profits, but they realize the potential for loss exists, and they keep their gambling stake within their financial means.

Then there is the other kind of gambler. This person risks more money than financially prudent, opening the door to potential monetary and personal disaster. For these players, their thrill in gambling comes from wagering amounts that involve significant risk to their financial well-being.

"When I gamble, I want to bet *significant money,*" is the way one out-of-control player described his behavior at the tables. "If I win, I want the bet to be big enough so it really *feels good*; and if I lose, the bet has to be big enough so it's *gonna hurt.*" Like the drug addict who seeks the ultimate high in the face of grave physical risk, gamblers who wager beyond their means seek the ultimate high in the face of grave financial ruin.

Can you be satisfied gambling within your financial means? Most of us want to bet enough to make the action exciting. And, certainly, a person who makes $50,000 a year might be expected to make larger bets than someone pulling in half that amount. That is why each of you must decide (based on *your* financial resources and obligations) what constitutes a "reasonable" gambling wager... a wager you can comfortably afford to lose.

Here are a couple of points that might assist you in keeping your betting limits financially prudent:

If you find that gambling is *not* exciting enough at your current betting levels and you can't really afford to raise your stakes, try to rekindle your gaming interest by gambling less often. Remember how school always seemed to be more exciting just after summer vacation? It was because you had been away from it for a while. The same holds true for casino gambling. If you cut back on your gambling trips and gambling sessions when on those trips, chances are your current wagering levels will regain some (or all) of their lost luster.

Sometimes a "change of game" can also perk up gambling interest, even at the same stakes. For example, after playing craps for many years, a $25 bet on the table didn't seem very exciting. Yet when I sat down to play blackjack or poker, a $25 bet seemed huge.

What happens if you try everything and *still* find that you're betting more than you can comfortably afford to lose? You might not like the answer I'm going to give you, but here it is.

> **If you find that your gambling excitement *only* comes from risking more than you can comfortably afford to lose, then don't gamble. Period. That kind of excitement just isn't worth the price.**

Dumb. Dumber. Dumbest. Three D's I don't want to see on your gambling report card. If you can avoid playing stupidly you're going to be a tougher player, a player with a better chance to win. Want to increase your winning chances even further? Then move on to the next section where you'll learn to harness your *psychological and physical* powers to create a *psychobiological* strategy for winning.

SECTION 4

The Four Psychobiological Keys To Winning In The Casino

"When my mind and body are both ready, that's when I hit the tables ready to win."

"Lowball" John Lowgren
Poker player

CHAPTER 8

Overcoming Your Psychological Governors

The term *psychobiological* might sound a bit fancy, but don't let the word mystify you. In the context of this book, it simply refers to the process by which you use your mind *(psycho)* and body *(biological)* to enhance your winning chances in the casino.

Regardless of where you decide to gamble or what game you choose to play, you must be in the proper mental and physical condition if you want to win. If you are not psychologically and biologically ready, you'll be battling yourself as well as the house... an altogether losing proposition. I've got some psychobiological techniques to get your brain and body in top shape for casino encounters. Let's go work out!

What Is A "Psychological Governor"?

Don't look for it in the dictionary, it isn't there. It is a term I created to refer to mental barriers that limit our gambling success to levels *less* than we are capable of achieving once these barriers are removed.

The concept of a "governor" is an interesting one. Those of you who are familiar with gas engines will know that a governor is a small, automatic, fuel-control device used to regulate speed. In automobiles, governors are also designed to restrict driving speed to some predetermined upper limit and—this is important—that limit is always *less* than the rate of speed obtainable by the vehicle without the governor in use. In other words, a governor on an automobile serves to reduce *performance below potential:* The car can't, in effect, work to its full capacity.

> A psychological governor does for gamblers what a mechanical governor does for an automobile: It restricts their range of performance and keeps their playing behavior below their playing potential.

There are three psychological governors we must identify, understand, and then disengage if we are to operate at peak gambling proficiency. Let's examine each one in turn.

Psychological Governor #1:

Negative Thinking

It's funny how insights seem to hit when you're least expecting them. Like after a tennis match. I was over at the public courts to work on my serve one day, when an old acquaintance named Jack sauntered up, said "Hello," and asked for a game. I agreed, hoping the competition would sharpen my play. As we rallied a bit to warm up, I noted with satisfaction that his strokes were smooth, his volleys crisp and sharp. It looked like I'd be getting some great experience because Jack had all the earmarks of a formidable foe.

Maybe too formidable. Four games into the first set I was down 3-1, and my opponent was stepping up to the service line. An ace and an easy put-away made the score 30-*love* and I had visions of a long afternoon. Then my seemingly invincible acquaintance made his first mistake— a double fault. That made the score 30-15, hardly a moment of great crisis for Jack, yet I could tell he was disturbed.

He fidgeted around for several moments before his next serve, rubbing his hands over the rim of his racket and wiping the handle against the side of his shorts. His next serve was a hummer, just wide. I signaled "out"... but Jack didn't seem to agree. He walked in a few steps, his face distorted in a scowl. "Are you sure?" he asked, in a tone of disbelief.

"It was out," I replied flatly.

"All right," he said, taking a deep breath. This time when he returned to the service line, he went through a whole series of gestures before he set himself for the serve.

"Long," I called.

This time the shot was clearly out, and Jack was clearly unhappy.

"Damn it to hell!" he cursed, causing a few heads to turn from the adjoining courts.

"You OK?" I asked, sensing his discomfort and trying to calm him down.

"Yes, damn it... toss me some balls," he shot back, making tight little circles around the baseline.

Jack's next serve was in, but there was nothing on it. I passed him and suddenly a 30-*love* game was add-out. I half expected an explosion from my opponent, but there was none. Instead, Jack stood a few feet from the net, hands on hips, glaring at his racket. Then, without saying a word, he returned abruptly to backcourt, and prepared for his next service.

The ball came at me as it had in the earlier games, a boomer serve that was almost by me before I got my racket on it. It was pure luck that I even returned the shot, and it was incredible luck that the ball stayed in... nicking the backline and bounding to a stop against the screening behind the court.

What could I say? It was a one-in-a-thousand shot. "Shouldn't have had it," I muttered, almost guilty over my sudden good fortune. Jack just stood, shaking his head, looking at the spot where the ball had hit the line.

"Service," I called, deciding that starting a new game might get things going and cool Jack down. Things got going but the only thing that got cooled down was Jack's game. What were once stinging forehands seemed like lobs—backhands that had kept me running seemed to follow me around like obedient children. It was the most incredible turnaround in a person's game I had ever seen.

I came back to win the first set 6-3, and was ahead 2-0 in the second when I decided to quit. Jack had turned on himself with a vengeance, and I just couldn't take any more of his self-abuse. As I began to walk off the court, Jack moved over to intercept me.

"Where are you going?" he asked. "The match isn't over yet."

"I know that," I replied, "but you don't need me. You play better against yourself than I ever could."

The Power Of Negative Thinking

It was on my way home from the match that I had my insight. I had been thinking about Jack's collapse and how weak-willed he must have been to fall apart the way he did. That's when the realization hit.

Jack was not weak-willed—no weak will could bring a skilled body to ruin that effectively, that completely. Regardless of what I thought about Jack's behavior, there was no doubt that he had a strong, well-developed will... *a will to lose.*

Unfortunately, this "will to lose" is not confined to competitive sports; there are thousands upon thousands of "Jacks" roaming through the casinos of the world, falling apart and losing at the tables, just as convincingly as my acquaintance did on the tennis court.

Many years ago, the well-known clergyman and author, Dr. Norman Vincent Peale, wrote an optimistic book extolling the virtues of *positive thinking*. His message was straightforward and simple: *If you believe, you can succeed.* Peale was convinced that if a person truly thought he could accomplish a given objective, he would... and considering some of the "impossible" feats performed by true believers—making miraculous medical recoveries, for example—Peale's convictions seemed reasonable. Such was the power of positive thinking.

Unfortunately, there is also the power of *negative thinking*, and it can wreak havoc with your chances of winning in the casino. **If one can believe and succeed, one can also *not* believe and fail, and therein lies the rub: Negative thinking can create a loser just as effectively as positive thinking can produce a winner.**

The negative-thinking gambler is a person with a psychological governor that can hamper his play at the tables. The more negative he is, the lower his psychological governor will be set. Put another way, the greater his negative thinking, the greater will be the gap between how well he is capable of playing and how well he actually plays.

Where Does
Negative Thinking Come From?

Negative thinking is a psychological governor that comes into being when we unconsciously place limits on ourselves—limits that we come to believe exist because we have been told they exist by some respected source such as our parents, peers, or teachers. Oftentimes, these limiting beliefs are instilled in us at an early age. One of the most effective methods I know to encourage the development of a powerful, lifelong, negative thinker is telling a young child again and again: "You're no good... you'll never amount to anything." With this kind of negative indoctrination, is it any wonder that many children *don't* amount to anything? They've been programmed to do poorly—to *think* they can't succeed—to *expect* they can't succeed... and their psychological governor is set for failure to make *sure* they won't succeed.

Sometimes, cultural expectations can serve to develop negative thinking in a whole class of individuals who are affected by such expectations. Take women, for example. Although the (false) belief that women are less intelligent than men is fading, it is still true in some cases that females are taught from earliest childhood that they cannot beat males in head-to-head competition. Is it any wonder that a woman poker player, raised under such cultural directives, often "clutches" in card games with men, suddenly discovering that her game has inexplicably gone to pieces?

Remember, people behave in ways consistent with the image they have of themselves, with the way they perceive themselves to be. If people think of themselves as losers, then they will gamble in a way that makes them losers. And then when they become losers, they will have proof they *are* losers, which makes them lose even more. To psychologists, it's a familiar cycle of the self-fulfilling prophecy.

We create our own psychological governors. We can also eliminate them: The losing cycle can be broken. If we are negative thinkers, if our ability to perform is being kept in check by a psychological governor, *we can do something about it*. We weren't born with this governor;

we created it (even though we weren't aware of this). And if we created it, then we can also destroy it, freeing ourselves to operate at full power: to perform to the limits that our potential allows.

Our minds are wonderful instruments at our command, far more complex and adaptive than any computer known to science. The attitudes you hold about yourself, about your ability—they needn't stay fixed, etched forever into your psyche. They can be changed, and will be, with some effort on your part. And this is true even for those people with very negative-thinking patterns. Ironically, it is these people—like Jack the tennis player—who have the *greatest* potential to change for the better. Think about it: If a person like Jack possesses a mind powerful enough to create such a potent psychological governor, then his mind is also powerful enough to wipe it away, to replace extremely negative thoughts with equally powerful, positive ones.

How Do You Know
If You're A Negative Thinker?

This is not always an easy thing to determine, particularly since these governors represent limits we *unconsciously* place on ourselves—often early in our childhood, when memories are sketchy and vague at best. At present there is no easy-to-take, valid test that can accurately tell us whether we are positive or negative thinkers. However, there are certain kinds of behaviors and outlooks that seem to be associated with negative thinkers. Read the following statements and think about them. Do they describe you?

First, in the realm of gambling:

1. When you sit down to play, you really don't expect to win, or you set your goal at breaking even.

2. If you start losing, you think you won't be able to come back.

3. If you start winning, you suspect you'll lose it all back.

4. In games of skill, you tend to lose against players who seem to be no more talented than you.

5. Your gambling has a tendency to fall apart if you make a few bad bets.

6. You tend to become self-abusive during play, particularly if things don't go your way.

7. In games of skill with a new opponent you know nothing about, you tend to assume you won't do that well.

8. In games of skill, if you lose to someone you're playing with for the first time, you figure you won't be able to beat that person the next time.

9. On an important roll of dice, or a pivotal hand of cards, you figure you're going to lose.

Now, here are some general statements about one's psychological outlook. How many of them sound like you?

1. You tend to have self-doubt rather than self-confidence.

2. You don't like to set difficult obstacles for yourself to overcome.

3. You feel that other people doubt your ability to perform adequately.

4. When it comes to your outlook on life, you are generally more pessimistic than optimistic.

5. You've probably met people whom you consider to be the confident type—people who have faith in themselves. You feel that you are not like them.

6. Your assessment of yourself tends to be generally more negative than positive; you tend to tear yourself down more than you build yourself up.

Overcoming Negative Thinking In The Casino

Getting people who see themselves as losers to enter a casino with a positive, winning attitude is no easy task. If their negative feelings are too pervasive and deeply rooted, it will take a major psychological overhaul in order to change them, which, of course, is well beyond the scope of this book. Fortunately, few gamblers are so negative about themselves that they cannot achieve a positive attitude. Here are some steps you can take to break through the psychological governor of negative thinking and gain an all-important psychobiological edge at the tables and slots:

1. Don't forget that we create our own psychological governors and we can also eliminate them. Sometimes simply realizing that psychological governors exist is all that is needed to break through them.

2. Play tough. Know the game you are playing, and play it smart. Play those games that give you the best statistical chance of winning. Also, learn how to counter the casino tactics designed to make you lose. Nothing builds a positive attitude like winning, so give yourself the best chance to beat the house.

3. Develop self-control at the tables. Knowing you can maintain self-discipline in the face of casino pressures will greatly enhance your self-confidence and potential for winning.

4. Do not play if you are currently residing in the "Dominion of the Dumbest" or are a compulsive gambler. Playing under these conditions will only fuel your losing ways and heighten your negative attitudes about yourself.

Winning Through Losing

All gamblers—even those playing skillfully at positive expectation games—will encounter losing sessions at the tables. In fact, by definition, if players never lose, then they wouldn't be gambling... as the term implies a component of risk in the wagering process.

Of course, very few players enjoy losing... it is a distinctly distasteful part of gaming; yet, if losing is viewed as an opportunity to learn rather than simply a failure to win, then something of value can be salvaged from the monetary setback.

Most important, losing acts as a forge in which we can temper our inner strength and sharpen our psychological edge. Winning won't do this nearly as well. As one veteran player observed: "If you want to learn what a person is really like, don't watch him when he's ahead, check him out when Lady Luck turns the other cheek."

Think back to your own gaming behavior and the actions of other gamblers you have observed. It is easy to display self-control, confidence, graciousness, and psychological strength when the cards and dice are going your way. The real test of courage, character, temperament, and self-esteem comes when Lady Luck turns on you with a vengeance.

In short, if winning can build profit, then losing can build character. It provides us with the opportunity to develop our inner strength and psychological resolve in the face of adversity. The Marines put it this way: "When the going gets tough, the tough get going."

Losing can also teach us how to win. It is said that the difference between a wise man and a fool is that the wise man makes a mistake but once. How often do you learn from your losses? If you're not learning, you're wasting a precious opportunity to do so.

Consider this analogy. A young man, in his early 20s, decided to take up the rather dangerous and taxing sport of rock climbing. After a tentative attempt to scale his first cliff, he made a painful discovery: Climbing over sharp rocks can lead to bumps, cuts, scrapes, and all forms of contusions on the human body. So what did he do? Before he undertook his second climb, he purchased shin guards, a helmet, some heavy clothes, and a better harness. This man *learned* from the losses he inflicted on his body and he took steps to reduce those losses in the future. What about you? When your bankroll gets bruised and tattered from the way you assault the casino coffers, do you make changes in your game plan so you can do better on your next trip? Do you take the steps necessary to protect yourself from a financial freefall or do you simply attempt to "climb the mountain" the same way as before, leaving the shin guards, helmets, and harnesses behind?

Think about it. The next time you lose, turn misfortune into good fortune. Use the losing session as a vehicle to build character and learn from your mistakes. That way you'll be winning through losing.

Psychological Governor #2:

Dysfunctional Superstitious Behavior

Bill is a high-rolling, fast-betting player. I met him one night at a Vegas casino and we exchanged small talk while shooting craps. Bill liked action. He'd bet the pass line and then place all the numbers—hoping the dice would stay out awhile before the inexorable 7 showed. It was poor percentage gambling, and Bill was paying the full price. For a half-hour his bankroll got torn apart; 7s seemed to be showing every four or five rolls. He just grimaced, signed more markers, and tried to weather the storm. "I'm waiting for the big hand," he explained, and put some more black chips on the layout. Well, the big hand *did* show. A well-dressed young man across the table began throwing number after number—the kind of hand designed to get Bill back on track... fast.

"The seven's gone to sleep," Bill chortled gleefully, and pressed his bets up.

The young man proceeded to make four straight passes, and that made Bill a true believer. Tossing in a handful of chips, he went for the chandeliers. "Sixty-four hundred across," he instructed the dealer, who put ten black chips on the 4, 5, 9, and 10, and twelve chips on the 6 and 8.

"Now let's have some numbers... *num*bers," Bill shouted, "You can do it, shooter."

"Eight... the point is eight," intoned the stickman as the young man came out on his fifth pass. Everyone was pushing bets out on the table, trying to ride the lucky hand to the hilt. A few more passes and everyone would be healthy, including Bill.

Then it happened. The young man tossed the dice with too much power, and one cube bounded off the table onto the casino floor.

"Die down... no roll," called the stickman.

Bill exhaled sharply. "Damn!" he exclaimed angrily, and turning to the dealer he said, "Take me down."

"What's the matter?" I asked.

"A die on the floor means a seven's at the door," he replied somberly, and watched as the shooter threw again... the point 10.

I glanced at Bill. He remained motionless.

The shooter threw two more numbers. If Bill had "stayed up" he would have made over $5,000. Bill looked miserable but he refused to bet. "I know a seven's coming," he muttered to no one in particular, "because the dice went off the table."

Bill was right. A 7 did come up. The only problem, from his point of view, was that it took twelve more rolls to do so—nine of which were point-numbers. Remaining out of action had cost Bill over $10,000!

Bill is not unique, you know. All over the world there are superstitious gamblers—individuals who believe their play can be influenced by factors that have absolutely nothing to do with their own competence or that of their opponents.

Normally, such beliefs are relatively innocuous human diversions. After all, what harm can come from a gambler wearing his "lucky shirt" to the tables, or refusing to roll the dice unless he first clicks them together three times? No harm—unless those beliefs affect the quality of his play.

I have seen competent blackjack and poker players come apart because they think they are jinxed. I have watched baccarat and dice players go from sensible to ruinous betting behavior because of a "sign." I have observed race and sports bettors abandon their thoughtful handicapping approach and wager on a horse or team because the name sounded right or the number matched someone's birthday. In these cases, superstitions and superstitious behaviors can be *very harmful*; in fact, they can sometimes bring about the downfall of otherwise tough players.

There is no room in a casino for dysfunctional superstitious behavior that reduces the gambler's winning potential. If you must cart a rabbit's foot around to the tables, go ahead. But don't go to pieces if you misplace the hairy appendage, and don't start making hare-brained bets because your lucky charm tells you to. Winners don't bet that way... and I want you to be a winner.

Superstitions Or Premonitions

I have met some interesting people in casinos, particularly at hot craps tables. Nothing seems to stimulate camaraderie and conversation like the disappearance of a 7 for 10, 20, even 30 consecutive rolls. It was during just such a hand that I met Linda.

She was playing next to me, showering the layout with chips and raking in a small fortune with each toss of the dice. After 18 straight numbers we were talking like old friends, laughing and congratulating each other on our good fortune. Then something strange happened. As the shooter reached for the dice to make his next throw, Linda's expression suddenly became tense. For a moment she just stood there, eyes wide, mouth half-open, then she blurted out, "My bets are off this roll!"

The boxman confirmed the betting change just before the shooter let the dice fly. A second later the wisdom of Linda's decision was confirmed. "Seven, line away," barked the stickman as a 4-3 showed on the dice.

Needless to say I was *very* interested in how Linda knew to call off her bets at just the right time. (I was also wondering why she didn't share the information with me!) I offered to buy her lunch, hoping the offer might loosen her tongue. I could have saved my money. Even before we got to the casino coffee shop she began sharing her "secret."

"I'll bet you're wondering how I knew a seven was coming up," she said, smiling proudly as we entered the restaurant.

"It crossed my mind," I admitted, trying to hear her words over the din of clattering dishes and the waitress who was calling us to a table.

"It's a feeling I get. When I get the feeling, I know a seven is coming up the next roll."

We sat down and I ordered two coffees. "This feeling," I said, "do you get it often?"

"It depends... but when I do, the seven always shows."

I scrutinized Linda's face carefully. On the one hand, she didn't look like a liar. On the other hand, she didn't look very wealthy, either—which she should have been if she could truly foretell the roll of the dice. After all, the ability to predict the outcome of an event before it occurred (called "precognition") would be all a gambler would need to bankrupt a casino in no time flat. I decided to press further.

"Do you get this feeling more than once during a gaming session?"

"Sometimes it might happen three or four times if I'm 'on.' I feel 'on' today."

That's all I had to hear. "Would you mind gambling with me after lunch and letting me in on the feeling when you get it? You know," I added, "I could have saved a lot of money if you had told me that 7 was coming out there."

Linda nodded her regrets. "I don't always get much chance to act when the feeling hits," she explained. "Yeah, come along... I owe you a shot at some casino money."

With that offer before me, I did all I could to hurry lunch along. Forty-five minutes later we were back at the tables. I decided to bet conservatively and see what would happen. For almost an hour Linda—and the dice—did nothing special. Then, with a guy at the other end of the table attempting to make a nine, my companion suddenly leaned over and said, "...Here comes the seven!"

"No action this roll," Linda informed the boxman.

"I put $10 on the come. The dice showed ace-deuce.

"I don't understand," Linda exclaimed. I thought I did, and lost $10 in the process.

Twice more during the afternoon Linda got the "feeling." One time a 7 did show, the other time it didn't. Linda wasn't impressed. Neither was I. She left the table muttering something about a "first time for everything."

I had another explanation. Linda, like many players I have known, was suffering from a severe case of *selective memory*. "Severe" in the sense that hers was an unusually bad case. "Selective" in the sense that whenever she "got the feeling" and a 7 showed on the next roll she remembered the event and was convinced she had psychic skill. On the other hand, if she got the feeling and the 7 failed to materialize, she "forgot" about it—not purposely, mind you, but forgotten it was, nonetheless.

Reading my explanation of Linda's behavior, far away from the tumult of the casino, you might find it hard to believe that a person could possess such a *selective memory*. Believe me, it is a lot more common than most people would care to admit. Although most players wouldn't be as extremely selective as Linda, most of us tend to remember when we were "right" and forget when we were "wrong": We tend to recall when a "hunch" worked and forget when it didn't. And that is how we come to mistake *selective memory* for *psychic ability*.

Selective Memory Can Affect Your Playing Effectiveness

Under normal circumstances, selective memory at the tables is a relatively harmless form of self-deception. But it can become extremely hazardous to a gambler's financial well-being if it starts to influence his or her betting behavior in deleterious ways. Example: A blackjack player has a $500 bet out. He is dealt a king-4 against the dealer's upcard of 6. Normally the player would stand, but this time he "feels" that a 7 is on top of the deck. He calls for a card and promptly busts with a 9. The dealer, it turns out, had a 16, and would have lost the hand had the player stood on his 14.

A few such "stupid" bets in a gambling day can make the difference between winning and losing at the casino. If you want to maintain your winning edge at the tables, it is vitally important that you *never* bet erratically on the basis of a "hunch" unless you truly *do* have psychic ability.

How Can I Tell if I Have Psychic Ability?

Precognition, the ability to predict the outcome of a gambling event before it occurs, is but one form of psychic ability. To my knowledge it has never been scientifically proven to exist under actual casino conditions. That doesn't mean that it doesn't exist or couldn't exist sometime in the future. It just means that it is highly unlikely that you or I possess it at this time.

If you want to see whether your "hunches" are truly psychic or simply a function of selective memory, perform this simple self-test.

1. Determine what form your hunch takes. For example, is it the ability to predict the fall of a card? To know when a slot machine is "hot"? To accurately call the roll of the dice?

2. Identify the conditions under which your know the "hunch" is present (is it a "feeling"? A voice telling you to bet?).

3. The next time(s) you gamble keep a pocket notebook and pencil handy. Then, each time you get your hunch, make a note on whether it turned out to be correct or incorrect. (For example, did the slot machine pay out or didn't it?) Do this *every* time you get the hunch and keep your records for a large number of hunches. This is important so you can be more confident that your results are not a function of normal statistical deviations. Once you have conducted your test, look over the findings and see whether your hunches did better than would be expected by chance alone.

An Example Of A Self-Test
For Psychic (Precognition) Ability

Let's consider Linda, the woman who thought she could predict when a 7 would be tossed. Using the three steps I have just outlined, Linda would be in a position to "test" the accuracy of her hunches. Standing at the craps table, she already knows what form her hunch takes (the ability to predict a 7) and the conditions under which the hunch is present (the "feeling" a 7 is going to show). Now she waits patiently for the feeling to occur. Every time it does she observes the next toss to determine if it is or isn't a 7 and enters the results in her pocket notebook. After recording these outcomes for a large number of "hunches" (let's use 114 for computational purposes), Linda is ready to test for psychic ability.

Based on mathematical probability, a 7 should (on the average) appear one out of every six rolls. Therefore, in 114 rolls, one can expect a 7 to show 19 times. If, upon examining her records, Linda discovers her hunch was right somewhere around 19 times, then she can be relatively certain her feelings *are not* indicants of true psychic (precognition) ability. Why? Because she should be able to guess the 7, by chance alone, 19 out of 114 times. As Linda's ability to predict the outcome of the roll improves beyond chance expectation (this can be determined by statistical testing), the possibility of psychic ability also increases, although other factors (too detailed to discuss here) could also be influencing the findings.

It is true that if you—as a gambler—can consistently predict the outcome of a gaming event at greater than chance levels, then you have the potential to win money at the tables. But before you go off and "bet the farm," I would keep two sobering thoughts in mind:

1. Because of selective memory, many people think they're psychic when they're not; and

2. No case of psychic ability has ever been demonstrated scientifically in the casino.

With these thoughts before you, I think you are in a better position to evaluate your hunches in an objective manner.

What About Intuition?

Some players tell me they don't necessarily believe they have psychic ability but still they do sometimes get "strong feelings" about what or which way to bet. "Should I follow my 'gut' feelings?" they want to know.

As long as "going with" your intuition doesn't cause you to wager in a manner that is scientifically unsound (for example, our blackjack player who hit a 14 against the dealer's upcard of 6) then I see nothing wrong with it. In fact, betting against "the way your feel" will probably make your gaming experience more unpleasant, which certainly should be avoided.

Oh... and one final thing: If, after analyzing your hunches, you find out that you *do* possess psychic ability take two critical steps: (1) Don't "reveal" your unique talent by winning so much so quickly that the casino management bars your from further play; (2) Please contact me through my publisher and let me verify your psychic ability by testing you in the casino!

Psychological Governor #3:

Thinking Unlucky

Evelyn Marie Adams is an interesting lady. One day she decided to take a gamble on the lottery in her home state of New Jersey. The result: a winning $3.9 million ticket. Wait, that's not the end of it. A short time later Ms. Adams purchased *another* winning lottery ticket, this time for $1.5 million.

If ever someone deserved to be described as lucky, Evelyn Marie Adams is indeed that person. Just how lucky was she? It is estimated that her double lottery win was a 17-trillion-to-1 shot! In other words, don't bet any serious money on it happening again in the near future.

My friend Randy had an interesting reaction to the Evelyn Adams saga. "Some people have all the luck," he grumbled. "If only I had a fraction of that woman's good fortune I'd have a shot at making it in life."

Is Randy right? Do some people have more luck than others? Are some of us destined to live on Jackpot Lane while others struggle vainly on Busted Flush Way?

Probably. But that's not the main problem. The main problem occurs when people like Randy spend so much of their time bemoaning their misfortune that they are in no position to take advantage of luck even if it hits them in the face.

Here's something every casino player should consider: No matter how unlucky you think you are, no matter how many times your performance seems to dip below statistical expectations, you *will* experience lucky streaks at the tables. I don't care if you lay claim to the title of "Born

Loser," you *can't* spend significant time at the tables or slots without experiencing periods of good fortune—the so-called "gambling rush." True, you might not be as lucky as often as Evelyn Adams, but you will have your moments of good fortune. I guarantee it!

It is very important that players believe they will experience lucky periods at the tables and slots. Otherwise they will psych themselves out to a point where they will not be able to recognize or take advantage of Lady Luck when she does smile their way. Furthermore, players who believe they are unlucky at the tables are in no mental condition to gamble effectively. The casino already has formidable tactics for beating the player, but none more powerful than players who step into a gaming establishment convinced they are already beaten.

Players who think they are unlucky play as though they are unlucky and, in a perverse sense of justice, create their own misfortune. Two examples come to mind. One involved a friend who was playing blackjack:

This individual had a large bet out when he was dealt two aces against the dealer's queen. I knew that the deck was favorable, so when he turned to me for advice I told him to split the aces. My friend refused. His reason? "I'm always unlucky when I split against a dealer's picture card."

The other example occurred at the craps table where I watched a player make five passes without increasing his bets. His companion asked him why he didn't press his bets to take advantage of the hot hand. "No way," explained the shooter. "I'm not lucky at this game." By the

way, the "unlucky" player made six more passes before
sevening out.

**People who believe they are basically unlucky seem
hard-pressed to maintain their psychological edge at
the casino. Typically, they:**

1. bet too conservatively when they are winning;

2. "steam" (increase their bets dramatically) when they
    are losing;

3. have difficulty weathering the inevitable losing streaks
    that all players experience.

Lady Luck is a wily woman. You can't buy her, you
can't fool her, you can't even get her on a schedule. But
you can court her. "Chance favors the prepared mind,"
is the way one scientist described the correct approach to
luck. For our purposes, the proper frame of mind is one
that recognizes the inevitability of both good and bad luck
at the tables and works to maintain psychological control
in either circumstance.

Put yourself in the proper frame of mind the next time
you visit your favorite casino. It's the best way to Lady
Luck's heart, and your best bet in any game you choose
to play.

PSYCHOBIOLOGICAL KEY #1

To enhance your winning chances, you need to disengage three *"Psychological Governors"*: (1) negative thinking; (2) dysfunctional superstitious behavior; and (3) thinking unlucky.

Perhaps you are a player who doesn't have any of the psychological governors just discussed. Consider yourself fortunate. However, you're not out of the psychobiological woods yet! Maybe you've got some character flaws that affect your play in a deleterious manner. Not sure? Read on.

CHAPTER 9

Eliminating The "AIR" Of Your Ways

"The only difference between a winner and a loser," observed Nick the Greek, "is character." That insight is as true today as it was during Nick's lifetime (1883-1966), and it will remain true as long as dice are tossed and cards turned.

Character. Nowhere is it manifested with more clarity and honesty than in the casino. For it is in the tumult of winning and losing that an individual's true nature is revealed, unmasked by the forces of elation and despondence that flow from the gaming experience. "What a man really is, and what he thinks of himself, seems to come out more swiftly at the gaming table than anywhere else," was the way Nick put it.

Unfortunately, when it comes to wagering, some players have character faults. Like diamonds they are flawed, and when put under the pressure of gambling, they crack. I'm now going to identify three of these character faults. If you have any or all of them, you'll need to correct

them if you want to increase your chances of winning in
the casino.

A = Arrogance

Arrogance is the first character fault that can lead to
poor play at the tables. Arrogance is *not* self-confidence.
In fact, self-confidence is a valuable asset when it comes
to gambling success. Players must have faith in their ability
to beat the house... or an opponent across the poker table.
However, that faith must be tempered by a realistic ap-
praisal of "enemy" strength. Self-confidence deteriorates
into arrogance when players act as if they are unbeatable,
failing to acknowledge (or respect) the strength of the
opposition.

Arrogant gamblers are often guilty of self-deception.
In an attempt to maintain an aura of indestructibility, they
will often exaggerate wins and underestimate losses. They
are also susceptible to "steaming" and often throw good
money after bad because of an unwillingness to pull back
against a clearly superior foe or a relentless losing streak.

It is not hard to recognize the arrogant gambler in action. This type of player is often loud, discourteous, and
boastfully reckless at the tables. Many times there is a
"macho" component to this individual's personality. In
men, this macho element often manifests itself in a tendency to bet higher and more aggressively, particularly
in the presence of women. Arrogant players also tend to
be storytellers and excuse-givers, inflating small wins into
monumental victories, and major losses into break-even
sessions.

Sadly, it is the nature of gambling and gamblers that many of us have our moments of arrogance. I certainly am no exception. Fortunately, there are always ways to combat "arrogant tendencies," and one of the best is a healthy dose of humility.

Unfortunately, humility isn't born into us like a breathing reflex. We have to learn it—and the lessons aren't easy to come by. For that reason I have decided to share with you my own lesson in humility.

My lesson took place during a trip to Singapore. At the time, I thought Americans were the only *real* high rollers; so when my hosts suggested that Chinese were big plungers, I didn't take them very seriously.

"Why don't you go to the casino and see for yourself?" they suggested.

I did. I took a plane to Malaysia and motored up to the Genting Highlands casino where a large number of Chinese were gambling with noteworthy zeal. I purchased a few hundred dollars in chips and made my way directly to the International Room, an area set aside for the alleged high rollers. Having been told that baccarat was the big money game in the Orient, I went over to the baccarat pit boss and said, "What are the betting limits?"

"Five hundred dollars, sir," was his reply.

I smiled. "Five hundred dollars? I thought you people catered to big players. A $500 maximum bet isn't much money at all."

The casino executive returned my smile. "I'm afraid you misunderstood me," he said, "It's a $500 *minimum* bet."

"Oh, yeah, right..." I stammered. My handful of chips suddenly felt woefully small and insignificant.

Chalk up one solid lesson in humility.

The next time you are at the tables feeling a little bloated on your own overconfidence, recall my story of the baccarat table with the $500 *minimum* bet. It might help you keep things in perspective. After all, a little humility is a healthy experience.

I = Impatience

Impatience is a second character flaw that can crack your bankroll wide open. Nowhere is the motto "patience is a virtue" more true than in the casino setting. It is true at the poker table where the player must learn to wait patiently for the correct hand to bet. It is true at roulette, craps, baccarat, and all the negative expectations games where gamblers must learn to conserve their bankroll during a bad run, waiting patiently for the tide to turn. And it is true in the race and sports book where the handicapper must learn to avoid making *snap* decisions and patiently consider all the important factors in making the *best* decision.

Impatience in the casino setting encourages poor decision-making and risky wagering behaviors. The impatient gambler at the tables behaves like the impatient driver on the highway. The only difference is that the gambler takes unnecessary risks with his bankroll while the driver takes unnecessary risks with his life.

Hank is a man who knows about patience and impatience. Let me tell you his story. Let it serve as an inspiration to you whenever you step inside a casino.

For several years I was involved in a weekly low-stakes poker game with a group of friends from the local area.

Nickel, dime, quarter action—a friendly game, nothing more. Yet, what the game lacked in money, it made up in ego. The participants were a competitive lot, and the importance of winning was reason enough to sustain a hotly contested game.

In my estimation, Hank was among the three strongest contestants in the game. He usually won, and sometimes he won the most at the table.

On one memorable Thursday evening we sat down to play at 7:30. Four hours and 15 minutes later, Hank left the game without ever winning a hand, even though he was involved in numerous pots. Think of it! The man didn't win one solitary hand in an evening of play. What makes this result even more remarkable is the fact that many of the pots were split (two winners per game).

Things started out where they had left off the following Thursday. Another hour-and-a-half of play passed and still Hank was winless, even though he continued to play a steady, sound game.

Then the losing streak ended. Hank began getting a "normal" run of cards, and he began to win. Patient and calm through his losses, Hank was ready to collect his share of pots when the cards began to go his way. In three additional hours of play he not only recouped all his losses of the previous Thursday, but pocketed an additional $30 in winnings as well.

What can we learn from Hank's poker experience? Consider this old gambling adage: "If you want to see how good a gambler really is, don't observe him when he's winning, watch him when he's losing." Put another way, a person's character is best revealed not in times of good fortune, but rather in times of adversity.

Hank experienced adversity all right: six hours of poker without a winning hand against players he normally beat with regularity. He could have become impatient, bet wildly, and lost his cool, waiting for that elusive pot to come his way. He did none of these things. He cut his losses, played with steadiness and intelligence, waited patiently, and was around to recoup his losses when, at last, the fall of the cards returned to "normal."

If you're going to sit down at the poker table—or any other gaming table for that matter—you're going to experience losing streaks. It's as simple as that. How you stand up under these trying times will, in large part, determine your overall success as a gambler. If, like Hank, you can face a string of losses with patience rather than *impatience*—with controlled rather than impulsive play— then you will be stronger mentally and financially for your efforts. If you can't, well at least you won't have to be impatient when it comes to losing your bankroll. *That* will happen plenty fast enough!

R = Rationalization

This third character flaw is a real danger for any gambler. It is the rationalizer who is most likely to practice self-deception... and succeed. This is the person who is always finding excuses to justify dangerous gambling behavior and finding reasons to explain away consistent losses.

Rationalizing gamblers make themselves believe that bad things can't happen to them in the casino. Like drunken drivers who convince themselves that "accidents only happen to other people," rationalizing players often don't see the error of their ways until the damage has already been done.

To be an effective player you must be honest with yourself when it comes to gambling issues. In the long run, self-deception turns into self-destruction. If you can avoid rationalizations in the realm of gambling, you'll be giving yourself a better chance to survive in the casino.

PSYCHOBIOLOGICAL KEY #2

Certain *character flaws* can affect a gambler's ability to win and should be corrected. Eliminate the "AIR" of your ways: **A**rrogance, **I**mpatience, and **R**ationalization.

CHAPTER 10

Using Biorhythms for Betting

Most people think of the body as a soft machine, a kind of mushy automobile. You take in fuel (food), wash it down the gas tank (throat), into the engine (stomach), where it combusts, giving off energy. Weight is considered to be an uncomfortable bulge in the superstructure; indigestion is simply the metal corroding. The body is acknowledged to grow and shrivel with age, but this is a long-term process that does not alter our view of ourselves, even when we become a vintage model.

In fact, the body is quite different from this stereotype. The human organism is a complex of interrelated, clocklike rhythms. These patterns vary so dramatically that a body that is in a particular physical state at noon may be in quite a different state just a few hours later. Says science writer Gay Luce: "Most people don't realize how much they change every 24 hours. They may notice that they get particularly tired at 2:00 p.m., or chilly in the late evening... but they remain largely unaware of changing immunity to infection or stress (which drops at night) or the fact that blood pressure, mood, pulse, respiration, blood sugar levels, and our ability to handle drugs all rise and fall in a circadian rhythm.

In the past 40 years, scientists have become increasingly impressed with the range and diversity in patterns of human behavior that seem to follow regular cycles or rhythms, called *biorhythms*.

The fact that the human body follows regular cycles enables us to predict what our physical and mental states will be at given times. If, for example, you note at what periods of the day you feel energetic and at what times you feel drowsy, a pattern will eventually emerge, indicating your daily alertness cycle. Once you identify your own biorhythms and their patterns, you can use this information to function more effectively on a day-to-day basis.

Consider this question:

What is the best time for you to gamble?

The answer: When you are psychologically and physically at your peak.

But when is that? Knowing your biorhythms can help answer this critical question.

To illustrate, let us assume that when you thought about your body cycles, you discovered that between 8:00 a.m. and noon you are drowsy, lethargic, dull, and easily distracted. Let us assume further that between 6:00 p.m. and 10:00 p.m. you are generally awake, active, alert and able to concentrate. When do you think it would be best to sit down and play blackjack or get into a fast-action craps game?

Pinpointing Your Biorhythms

When you want to discover what your biorhythms are, it is valuable to use a method known as *body charting*. This is simply a log or diary for recording and keeping track of your hourly, daily, monthly, and even yearly body rhythms. It is sometimes true that fluctuations in some body rhythms are so readily apparent to us that we needn't chart them to know when they're most likely to occur. "I'm an early riser—have been all my life," might be the observation of a person who knows his body cycles when it comes to sleeping-waking patterns. If this is true in your case, then simply being aware of the patterns and their fluctuations will be sufficient to take advantage of them.

Yet, in many cases, we are unaware of our body cycles—or inaccurate in assessing them—and under these conditions body charting is the best way to uncover them and the information they provide. Fluctuations in our moods, for instance, are often difficult to spot without the aid of body charting. So are changes in our physical responses such as energy level and reaction time, when the cycles for these bodily states are irregular or of long duration.

Fortunately, body charting does not require elaborate machinery. Simply decide what mood or physical state you wish to chart, then keep track of its occurrence on a piece of paper, in a diary, or on any other recording device. The technique is simple, practical, and available to anyone with a pencil, paper, and a little patience.

Your Gambler's Body Charting
(Biorhythm) Diary

There are many ways to chart your body cycles as well as many different cycles you could choose to chart. What I want to do is make your task as inexpensive, convenient, and simple as possible, while concentrating on those biorhythms that will help you play when your *psycho* (psychological) *biological* (physical) skills are at their peak.

To do this, please turn your attention to the sample diary page that I have provided. Note that there are seven biorhythms you should focus on: *energy, concentration, tension level, intellective function, level of self-confidence, wakefulness, and mood*. These are the biorhythms I feel are most important in determining your best time to gamble. However, feel free to alter this list (add or subtract biorhythms), if you feel there are more relevant biorhythms affecting your gaming behavior.

Sample Page From
A Gambler's Body Rhythm Diary

Date _____ Time _____ Chart # _____

Energy

Lethargic _____ Active

Concentration

Easily _____ Able To
Distracted   Focus Attention

Tension Level

Tense _____ Relaxed

Intellective Function

Sluggish _____ Sharp

Self-Confidence

Insecure _____ Confident

Wakefulness

Fatigued _____ Awake

Mood

Bad Mood _____ Good Mood

One hour after you awaken, and every three hours thereafter until bedtime, evaluate your moods and physical states as listed in the diary. Use a new sheet for each evaluation. If you feel that filling out the diary every three hours is too much of a hassle, then wait for longer intervals before filling it out (say every four, five, or six hours). There is no magic number of times you should make entries in your diary; what is important is that you generate sufficient data points for accurately mapping the biorhythms in question.

Some people have trouble filling out their body rhythm diary because they're unclear about the definitions of the various moods and physical states listed in the diary. This is not surprising, as these terms have many different meanings to different individuals. For our purposes, utilize the definitions that follow when filling out your Body Rhythm Diary.

1. *Energy:* Refers to the amount of physical zest or pep you have. When you feel run-down or physically drained, your energy level would be low *(lethargic)*. When you feel charged and full of gusto, your energy level would be high *(active)*.

2. *Concentration:* Refers to the ability to zero in on an activity and keep it at the center of your attention. When you are unable to focus your attention successfully, your concentration level would be low *(easily distracted)*. When you are able to rivet your attention, your concentration level would be high *(able to focus attention)*.

3. *Tension Level:* Refers to the amount of nervousness you feel. When you feel loose, calm, and mentally at ease, your tension level would be low *(relaxed)*. When you feel uneasy, under stress, and jittery, your tension level would be high *(tense)*.

4. *Intellective function:* Refers to how well you can use your mind at a given point in time. When you can't seem to think clearly, quickly, or creatively, your intellective function would be low *(sluggish)*. When your mind is in high gear and thinking has clarity and power, your intellective function would be high *(sharp)*.

5. *Self-confidence:* Refers to how much you believe in yourself—how much self-assurance you have. When you have faith in your decisions and believe you can take on the world, your self-confidence would be high *(confident)*. When you doubt your ability to succeed and question your worth, your self-confidence would be low *(insecure)*.

6. *Wakefulness:* Refers to the degree of alertness you are experiencing at a given time. When you feel drowsy or tired, your wakefulness level would be low *(fatigued)*. When you feel wide-awake—"bright-eyed and bushy-tailed"—your wakefulness level would be high *(awake)*.

7. *Mood:* Refers to your general disposition—how you are feeling at a given time. If you are happy and in good spirits, your mood would be positive *(good*

mood). If you feel sad and rather low, your mood would be negative *(bad mood).*

Here's an example of how to make an entry into your diary. We'll use the "energy" question for illustrative purposes. If, at approximately 2:00 p.m., you feel more lethargic than is customary for you during a normal waking day, then you would put an "X" on the left side of the continuum, This would indicate that you had "less energy than normal." *"Normal"* refers to the average level of energy you usually experience from day to day. In other words, if at 2:00 p.m. you feel much less energy than normal, you don't mean as compared to other days at 2:00 p.m., but rather to what your normal energy level is over the entire day.

By duplicating the Diary sample page for the number of days you plan to plot your biorhythms, you can construct your personalized diary (number the pages consecutively and use new ones each time you make an entry).

You'll get the most out of a body rhythm diary if you use it correctly. Here are two important points to keep in mind as you begin your body charting:

1. *Length of diary:* "How many days should I chart my body cycles?" This is a question I am frequently asked. Some cycles are more difficult to track than others (they are of longer duration, making trends more difficult to spot). A rule of thumb is that a good sampling should cover a period of 90 days. The minimum acceptable time limit is 30 days.

2. *The backward glance:* Once you have completed an individual diary page, do not look at it again until you have completed all of the pages and are ready to tally your results. If you do look back, you may unconsciously alter your answers to fit ideas of what you think your biorhythms should be.

When you have charted your body rhythms for a suitable period of time, go back over the data points to see if any patterns emerge. If you find that some of your moods or physical states do change with predictable regularity, then you will be in a position to use that information in determining your best time(s) to gamble. If, for example, you find that a majority of your physical states tend to "peak out" at regular intervals during the day, you could then schedule casino visits to take place at these times. You could also discover, upon examining your diary pages, that your physical states peak out for two or three days at a time and then recede for weeks.

Again, you could take advantage of this harder-to-recognize physical pattern by bunching your gambling activities into your two-to-three-day "up" periods.

Some individuals use their body rhythm charts in quite a different fashion. They fill out a chart each time before they gamble, then compare their gaming results with the data on their charts. What they are looking for is any pattern of responses in their diaries that corresponds to their pattern of winning or losing at the tables.

For instance, assume that after numerous chart entries and gambling sessions, players were able to determine that the best winning sessions usually occurred when their various moods and physical states were close to normal.

This might suggest that the best bet would be to gamble when the player's moods and physical states were not extreme in either the positive or negative direction.

If you decide to use your body rhythm charts in this manner, do so with a healthy skepticism concerning the results. Remember that correlation is not causation, and that any relationships you find should be thoroughly tested at the tables to make sure they are valid and not due to chance factors.

When you first begin using your body-rhythm diary. it might seem like too much of a hassle. Give it a chance— it can be an intriguing adventure. Most of us are so out-of-touch with ourselves that any extensive attempt at self-observation produces many unexpected and useful insights. Most important, if you undertake a diligent program of body charting, you will gain an additional tool for harnessing your psychobiological powers in your battle against the casino.

PSYCHOBIOLOGICAL KEY #3

Our behavior is regulated by interrelated, clocklike rhythms know as *biorhythms*. We can use knowledge of our biorhythms (learned through "body charting") to pinpoint our best time(s) to gamble. Knowing your biorhythms won't guarantee gambling profits, but it will help you play when your physical and psychological skills are at their peak. And that's an edge worth having.

Biorhythms In Action:
Spacing Your Gambling Trips For Maximum Playing Effectiveness

The year was 1975. Atlantic City gambling didn't exist. If you wanted to visit a legal casino in the United States it was Nevada or nothing. Living in Florida made a Nevada holiday a major trek for me, and an expensive, time-consuming one at that. All of which meant I couldn't get to Nevada often enough—or stay long enough—to satisfy my gambling desires.

I decided to do something about my problem. In August of 1975, I scheduled an open-ended gambling trip, with no set return date. Where my previous gaming excursions had lasted no longer than three days, this trip was to last as long as it took me to lose or to double my bankroll. That, I decided, would give me sufficient time and action to satisfy my gambling appetite once and for all.

I was very excited when the trip finally got underway. The moment my plane touched down at McCarran I hit the tables. I gambled up and down the state, from Vegas to Reno to Tahoe and back to Vegas. For ten days it was non-stop wagering.

Then something strange happened. For the first time in all my years of gambling, I lost the sense of exhilaration that always came with play at the tables. I even found myself looking around Vegas for things to do *outside* the casinos. I returned home, amazed by the feelings I had experienced.

Then something stranger happened.

By 1980, I was able to afford more frequent trips to the casinos. This was due, in part, to my higher income and also to the opening of Atlantic City gaming establishments nearer my home. Yet, even though my gaming skills increased with more frequent trips (I got sharper at the tables with more practice), I still found myself a loser at the end of most casino visits.

It took me a while to sort things out, but when my experiences of 1975 and the early '80s finally sank in, I realized something vital: **Gambling (at least for me... and I suspect for you as well) was an appetite, like a desire for food. And, like a desire for food, my appetite for gaming tended to increase the longer I went without it and decrease the more I had of it.**

Before 1975, I had never had my fill of gaming. Like a person on a subsistence diet, I didn't realize that one could reach a saturation point at the tables. Then came ten days of non-stop play and I experienced gambling *boredom* for the first time. A binge of concentrated play had ended my hunger to play.

Of course, my gambling desire resurfaced after a suitable absence from the casino. But in the early 1980s, when I gambled on a more frequent basis, my level of desire was never as strong as during the more infrequent trips of the 1970s. Because I didn't realize that increasing gambling frequency was the cause of this reduced desire, I tried to "jack up" my sagging gambling excitement by wagering more recklessly and with larger bets.

This is why I began experiencing more losing trips. To make up for the gambling excitement that was lost because of more frequent visits, I was taking more risks, taking deeper plunges at the tables. I was like the person who had gone from a subsistence diet to a regimen of regular meals, and was now growing fat because I chose to eat richer, tastier food in an attempt to maintain the "thrill of eating" that scarcity had once guaranteed.

What did I learn from analyzing my gambling trips? That too much *or* too little gambling negatively affected my performance in the casino. When my gambling trips were infrequent, my excitement level was too high to wager effectively. Conversely, when my gambling trips were too frequent, my excitement level was too low to optimize my betting behavior.

Charting My Optimal Time To Gamble

Once I realized that the frequency and length of my gambling trips influenced my desire to gamble and, consequently, the skill of my wagering, I took steps to space my casino visits for maximum enjoyment and playing performance. I did this by varying the length of time on and between gambling trips, trying out different schedules until I found the one that was best for me. It turned out that a gambling trip every three months was optimal. If I visited casinos more frequently I became bored more easily—and tended to bet bigger and more wildly to put the "zing" back into the action. On the other hand, if I waited much beyond three months, I was so hungry for play that I tended to bet out of control to "make up for lost time" and satisfy my gambling hunger, much like a starving man might attack a smorgasbord after days without food.

What does this all mean for you? You should attempt to space *your* gambling trips so as to optimize your success in the casino. This is particularly true if you must travel a significant distance or incur significant expense to get to a gambling destination.

Each individual has his or her own unique biorhythm for gambling: the ebb and flow of desire to play in a casino. You'll want to discover your own particular rhythm and then use this information to schedule your casino visits accordingly.

> Gambling too frequently or infrequently: both approaches can reduce your playing effectiveness. If you want to maintain your psychobiological edge at the tables you'll need to space your gambling trips at appropriate intervals; intervals that allow you to enter the casino when your desire to gamble is *moderate,* rather than too high or too low.

We have now explored three psychobiological keys to winning at the tables. Our fourth and final key will also help you in your quest to beat the casino... and it might even save your life!

CHAPTER 11

Winning Your Wager Against Excessive Stress

There are few activities in life that are as compelling as gambling. In fact, some of the things people will go through to keep "in action" are almost beyond belief. Recall, if you will, the players who gambled on through floods, fires, and medical emergencies in Chapter 3.

Which brings us to an important point. **Gambling, by its compelling nature, is stressful. Win *or* lose, the person wagering at the tables is in a heightened state of agitation; heart pumping, adrenaline flowing, brain at full alert. Faced with the stress inherent in gaming activities, it is vitally important that the player learn the techniques to keep that stress within healthy (not excessive) bounds.** This is vital for maintaining the psychobiological edge so necessary to good health and winning play at the tables.

Healthy Stress Vs Excessive Stress

When I emphasize the need for reducing excessive stress in your gambling and your life, some of you might assume that I am recommending the elimination of stress altogether. This is not the case. Normal amounts of stress never hurt anybody; in fact, moderate amounts of stress can actually enhance performance and make for a more meaningful, exciting life.

It is fair to assume that one of the major reasons people do gamble is to create stress—to get, as a famous high-stakes gambler has been known to say, the "zings" and "stings" of casino action.

Gambling "action" that serves to arouse and excite the player is good, in proper doses. But like many beneficial activities, too much of a good thing can lead to undesirable (even tragic) consequences. Stress becomes dangerous when it becomes excessive, forcing the body to run like a car with the accelerator stuck to the floor. When we become stressed, our bodies shift into a state of high physical arousal preparing us for the so-called "fight-or-flight" response. If we experience this state too often, or stay in it too long, we will eventually break down like any overworked machine.

Thus, gambling should be seen as a stimulant, but one that doesn't get out of hand. The problem, as we've already learned, is that most casinos have been designed to encourage excessive, rather than moderate, levels of stress; a fact that can be debilitating to your bankroll *and* your body. What can you do about this? You'll know once you understand...

The "U-Curve" Arousal Function

At the beginning of the 20th century, two men by the name of Yerkes and Dodson formulated a "Law" of human behavior. It states that an inverted "U-curve" relationship exists between a person's level of *arousal* and his or her *performance;* that is, performance is best under *moderate* levels of arousal and decreases as arousal levels get too low or too high.

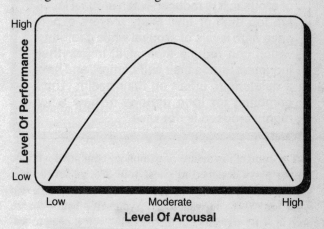

The "inverted U-Curve" relationship between
level of arousal and level of performance.

What the figure shows us is that people perform best under moderate levels of stimulation. As the tapering curve indicates, performance deteriorates if there is too little or too much arousal. Too little arousal, and an individual becomes bored, apathetic, unmotivated. Too much stimulation, and that person becomes overloaded, overworked, overstressed, overwhelmed.

The U-Curve Arousal concept is important for both our health and our success in casinos throughout the world. Decisions concerning when and how long we gamble should always be made with an eye to playing during *moderate* (as opposed to high or low) levels of arousal.

> **Gambling performance is maximized when the player is experiencing *moderate* levels of arousal; it is reduced when arousal levels are too high or low. Many players experience *high* levels of arousal while gambling, which can reduce their skill, impair their judgment, erode their self-control, and have a deleterious effect on their health. Thus, gambling for long periods of time when highly aroused is not wise.**

The compelling nature of gambling, combined with the casino ploys designed to boost your arousal levels, is a potent combination that can knock out your wealth *and* your health. If you want to give yourself a better chance to win—and stay alive in the process—you'll need to follow certain rules designed to keep your gambling within the boundaries of moderate, rather than excessive, stress. Observing these rules will require a little planning and scheduling *before* you begin gambling, and a lot of self-control once you *start* gambling.

When you first begin using these rules in the casino you might feel they are limiting your gambling spontaneity, and putting undue restrictions on your action. Don't despair—these feelings will pass. In fact, once you follow the rules on a regular basis, you'll enjoy your gambling more than ever... because you'll win more, lose less, and feel physically better in the process.

1. Set up a gambling schedule before you embark on a trip to the casino and stick to the schedule once you start play.

2. Do not gamble more than three or four times a day.

3. Do not gamble more than an hour at a time.

4. If it takes longer than three hours to reach a gaming destination, try to avoid play immediately after you arrive. Give your body and mind a chance to adjust to the new environment. Also, be wary of jet lag if you've flown across several time-zones to reach the casino.

5. Try to make your pattern of sleeping-waking hours the same for a gambling trip as you would for any other away-from-home vacation. This is probably one of the most important rules for defending against *stimulus bombardment* (discussed in chapter 3), and one of the most difficult to observe. Remember that most casinos have been designed to encourage round-the-clock action—exactly the kind of schedule that will disrupt your biorhythms, encourage excessive stress, and be detrimental to the health of your body and your bankroll. Don't fall victim to these casino temptations. You wouldn't stay up for 24 hours straight visiting Yellowstone or London; don't do it in Vegas or Atlantic City, either.

6. Don't gamble immediately after a heavy meal.

7. Don't gamble while under the influence of drugs or alcohol.

8. Don't gamble when you feel "stale," tired, listless, or rundown.

9. Stop gambling immediately if you feel hassled or emotionally distraught for *any* reason.

10. Don't gamble when you feel sick.

11. Don't gamble with people who affect your play in a negative manner.

12. Don't gamble when you find it difficult to concentrate.

13. Don't jam too many activities into your day. Give yourself adequate "breathing room." The last thing you want to be is tense and rushed during a gambling trip. I have seen people schedule two—even three— shows a night when in Las Vegas, running all over town trying to keep up with their reservations. Then they try to gamble. It's no wonder they play so poorly... and end up feeling poorly, too.

14. It is helpful to keep physically active during gambling trips. It keeps the mind and body alert... and gives a person the opportunity to get rid of some of the tensions built up through the stress of gaming.

For this reason I like to schedule walks throughout my gambling trips. (If the weather is bad at your gambling destination, you can always walk the corridors of most major shopping malls.)

15. Look in a mirror before *each* gambling session. If you appear "wired or tired" stay away from the tables. Why risk your money and your health when your psychobiological condition makes you more likely to lose? Go with the strategy expressed by poker player John Lowgren at the outset of this chapter: "When my mind and body are both ready, that's when I hit the tables ready to win."

16. Last but certainly not least... get in the habit of eating right: Ease up on the junk ford, eat a well-balanced diet, and enjoy your meals if for nothing more than timely, relaxing breaks from the tables.

Healthy Body, Healthy Mind, Makes You The Effective Gambling Kind!

How many times have you been guilty of any or all of the following actions during a gambling trip?

1. You gamble hour after hour, not taking breaks to give your mind and body some rest.

2. You eat too much or too little... often rushing through your meals to get back to the action.

3. You play for days with minimum sleep, or no sleep at all.

4. You live your gambling trip like there is no tomorrow: jamming as many activities as you can into as little time as possible.

5. You drink too much.

6. You play on, even when you're not feeling well or are mentally uneasy or unhappy at the tables.

When you play under conditions, in which you are not physically or mentally at your peak, you are endangering your financial and bodily health. Why take such risks? Gambling can be so much more fun, profitable, and healthy when we are strengthening rather than compromising our psychobiological well-being.

Our minds and our bodies are not separate entities, they work together to optimize our performance and quality of life. When we undertake a lifestyle that compromises our psychobiological system, we are reducing our chances at the gaming *and* mortality tables.

Moderation: The Key To Optimizing Our Psychobiological Power

After decades of scientific research and anecdotal evidence, it is clear that *excess* is the enemy of psychobiological well-being, and *moderation* is its ally. At first glance, a life of moderation might sound like a life of boredom, but this need not be the case. Moderate amounts of food and drink, moderate amounts of exercise, moderation in the way we gamble and have fun... all this can be satisfying without being excessive. Living in the fast lane leads to break-downs and a dulling of the senses.

The human body was not meant to remain in high gear hour after hour, day after day. A life of excess creates excessive stress, which, in engineering terms, is a "force that tends to deform a body." And that's what excessive stress does to our bodies in unhealthy, crippling ways.

Moderation in the way we live is not a prescription for tedium; rather, it is a strategy for living longer, stronger, and more successfully... at home, at work, and *in the casino*. Moderation is the mark of a winner!

Win your wager against excessive stress. It's worth the effort.

Make it so!

SECTION FIVE

The Four Death Sentences In A Casino... And What You Can Do To Overturn Them

Do not speak such terrible words; ugly consequences will surely follow.

Anonymous

CHAPTER 12

Death Sentence #1:

"I Didn't Come All The Way Out Here To Break Even."

Have you ever been out in public—pretty well minding your own business—when suddenly you overhear a stranger say something you badly want to challenge? It happens to me in casinos all the time, particularly when I hear players making pronouncements that are tantamount to "death sentences" for their bankrolls.

Of course, I don't say anything. It would be rude... and besides, some gamblers don't cotton to criticisms of the way they play. Nevertheless, I thought you might be interested in hearing some of these tragic comments... and my reactions to them. If you want to survive as a player—if you want to experience winning trips to the casinos—then these are four death sentences you will never want to impose on your gambling stake. Unless, of course, you believe in capital punishment... your own capital, that is!

Let's take a look at Death Sentence #1:

Ted is a friend of mine from Florida. He's into real estate and construction. He's also into casino gambling, making four trips a year to Vegas in search of wealth at the baccarat tables.

Recently, I spotted Ted at a posh Strip casino. He was moving from the bell desk to the casino floor at a rapid pace, a wad of hundred-dollar bills spread like a fan in his left hand.

"Hey, Ted," I shouted, waving my arms to get his attention. "Where's the fire?"

"My plane leaves in a few hours... I've got time for just one more shot."

"Well, it looks like you got 'em good this time," I observed, pointing to Ted's bankroll as I caught up with him.

"This?" Ted snorted, slapping at the bills with his free hand. "This," he explained, "is what I started with."

"How long have you been here?"

"Four days," Ted replied.

"Four days and you've still got your total bankroll? I'd say that's pretty good." Then, against my better judgment, I tendered a suggestion.

"Ted, why not quit now while you still have all your money? That way you can come back next trip with your stake intact and gamble when you're not in such a hurry."

Ted pulled up short and gave me an "are-you-crazy" look. "You've *got* to be kidding!" he exclaimed. *"I didn't come all the way out here to break even."*

The Danger Of Long-Distance Gambling

Ted has a problem which is epidemic amongst players who must travel a long distance to reach their gambling destination: the need to either win or lose during each trip. In fact, this tendency is so strong I feel safe in creating this gaming "law."

Casino players are more likely to reject the alternative of "breaking even" on a gambling trip...

1. the further they must travel to reach a gaming location (particularly if air travel is involved);

2   the longer a person must wait between gambling trips; and

3. when incidental costs such as food, transportation, and lodging, represent a significant portion of the gambler's bankroll—15 percent or more.

Ted provides the perfect profile of a player who suffers from the "I didn't come all this way to break even" syndrome. He doesn't have unlimited gaming funds, so he restricts himself to four gambling trips a year. The trip involves six hours of air travel, plus a significant outlay of out-of-pocket expenses for transportation, hotel, meals, etc. Thus, when Ted hits the tables, he feels he must reach a decision in his contest with the casino—after all, he reasons, he has come too far and spent too much time and money to be satisfied with a draw. Besides, breaking even is psychologically dissatisfying he rationalizes, like a tie game in hockey or soccer.

The Folly Of Ted's Approach

Of course, Ted is not totally correct when he assumes he has "tied" the casino when he ends a trip with his bankroll the same size as when he began. In fact, he has *beaten* the tables when you consider that his game, baccarat, has a negative expectation for the player. Considering the thousands of dollars in bets that Ted made over the length of his stay... he is, in reality, a winner against the casino advantage. He has enjoyed hours of gaming in luxurious surroundings—at no gambling cost to him.

Yet, the "gambling-at-no-cost" argument is not the best reason to willingly end a gaming trip in a break-even position. The best reason is to maintain your psychological edge in the casino. Taking a final fling at the tables with a plane to catch is an absolutely *terrible* time to gamble, possibly rivaling the time at the beginning of a trip when the arriving player dashes from airport to casino for immediate action. Here are the dangers you face when you take a final shot at the tables to break a tie with the house:

1. If you are in a time bind—your plane leaves in two hours, for example—your concentration and judgment will most likely suffer. Playing under pressure—any kind of pressure—tends to weaken your skills and your gaming resolve.

2. Knowing that this is your final gaming session—and that you will have to wait a long time before the next one—encourages reckless, "dramatic" betting. You want action, big action, to "hold you over" until your next trip. And because you have already been in ac-

tion for several days, chances are you'll need bigger wagers to keep the excitement level perking.

3. You are coming to the table with a "winner take all" mentality. This is your showdown session with the house. Unfortunately, under these circumstances, the tendency is not to be satisfied with a small loss or gain but, rather, only a decisive victory or defeat will fill the bill. Thus, for example, if you have allotted yourself $5,000 for five days of gambling ($1,000 per day) and you are even, the tendency is to suddenly be willing to risk the entire $5,000 in the showdown session.

"After all," you reason, "isn't that how much I brought out here to gamble with?"

Here's my suggestion for overturning this death sentence:

The next time you find yourself even with the casino on the final day of a gaming trip, *don't hit the tables* on your way out the door. Do this: Tell yourself that if you don't spend the money now, those funds will be available for the next trip. Or remind yourself that when you break even in a casino, you're actually a winner. You've beaten the house advantage and had great action... for *free*. And don't forget the most important break-even benefit of all: When you're willing to leave the tables with a "tie" in hand you won't have to worry about losing your shirt along with it! You've demonstrated a remarkable mental toughness in the face of casino temptations and that, in itself, is a victory worth celebrating.

CHAPTER 13

Death Sentence #2:

"Wait Here A Moment While I Make A Bet To Cover Dinner."

This story is true. A premium junket player has just finished his gaming for the day and heads into the gourmet restaurant for a comped meal. The bill comes in at just under $100, but the only cost to the player is a $25 tip to the waiter. As he leaves the restaurant to catch an evening show, the gambler must walk through the casino where a roulette wheel catches his attention. "Hey, I might as well get my tip money back" he thinks to himself... pulling out a Franklin and placing it on "black."

One spin later the ivory ball sits in 14-red and our well-fed friend is out a $100 bill... and the $25 tip. Undaunted, he puts two more hundreds on the "black" to "get a winner for after dinner." I'm sure you can guess the sad ending to this gaming encounter. An hour later the player is stuck for a $10,000 marker, the $25 tip, *and* a serious case of indigestion. And the saddest part of the story is the player had finished his gambling for the day *before* dinner. Had he not tried to chase that $25 tip, he would have $10,000 in the cage instead of the casino's coffers.

Sadly, the story of the junket player (with slight variations) occurs all too frequently in gaming establishments throughout the world. Even players who are normally well-controlled have been known to drop bundles in ill-advised attempts to recoup incidental expenses (e.g., food costs, hotel bills, cab fares, tips) incurred on gambling trips. I myself have fallen victim to this affliction—one time losing $1,500 in an attempt to recover an $8 cab fare.

It seems there are many psychological reasons for trying to recoup incidental expenses at the tables. One player told me that he hated to spend money for anything but gambling when he was in Vegas, and that's why he felt compelled to cover non-gaming expenses at the tables. Other gamblers have spoken of the need to get even when they fall behind in out-of-pocket expenses. Some players even argue that it is bad luck to spend money on incidentals and not try to win it back in the casino.

In addition to players' psychological reasons for this ill-advised approach to gaming, *casino placement encourages gambling to recoup incidental expenses*.

Casino operators know their livelihoods depend on gaming revenue. They also realize that gamblers have a tendency to try to recoup their incidental expenses at the tables. For this and other reasons they have made their casinos the *focal point* of action, the *hub* of activity. We discussed this "casino as a focal point" concept extensively in Chapter 3.

Recall the plight of our ill-fated junket player. He had to pass through the casino on his way from the restaurant to the showroom. Had he not been required to take such a routing, it is unlikely he would have sought out the roulette wheel to recoup his $25 tip. After all, he had finished gambling for the day. In the end, the experience of the junket player underscores the wisdom of the casino operators in placing their gaming establishments at the crossroads to everywhere.

My suggestion for overturning this death sentence is easy. **The best approach to *"incidental expense"* wagers is to eliminate them—pure and simple.**

Unfortunately, it ain't that easy. Many players have great difficulty resisting the temptation to recoup non-gaming expenses at the tables and slots. If you're one of those individuals, don't despair. There are still things you can do to reduce the frequency or intensity of such temptations during your gambling trips:

1. The best recommendation is to arrange your gambling trips so there will be a minimum of out-of-pocket expenses once you arrive. This can be done by pre-paying the trip in advance, going on a junket, or signing for everything and paying the total bill as the *last thing you do* before returning home.

2. If you must pay incidental expenses during your trip:
    (a) *Try to put them on credit cards* (preferably those that don't offer cash advances). There is more of a temptation to "get the expenses back" if you use chips or money. (After all, you can pay the credit card charges when you return home... leaving your bankroll intact for play at the tables.)

(b) *Try to avoid contact with casinos for as long as possible after such a transaction takes place.* (The longer the interval, the better the chances you won't feel compelled to "get the money back" by betting at the tables.)

(c) *Be sure to keep your incidental expenses separate from your gambling bankroll.* In other words, if you intend to spend $1,000 for gambling, be sure to bring enough extra money to cover *all* incidental expenses *without* having to dip into the $1,000 bankroll.

The next time you take off for your favorite casino, make a pledge to avoid any gambling designed to recoup incidental expenses. That way your next cab ride won't end up costing $1,500!

CHAPTER 14

Death Sentence #3

"Take My Bags Upstairs...
I Want To Check Out The Casino
Before I Go To My Room."

If you look forward to your gambling trips as much as I do, then I know you will be familiar with the following scenario:

Your flight has just arrived at your casino destination—let's say, Las Vegas—and you can already feel the adrenaline surging through your body. You hustle off the plane to the sounds and sights of your gambling playground: the slots, the sounds of money, the delighted shouts of the winners. Winners like *you* are going to be.

You walk briskly to the baggage claim, wait impatiently for your suitcase, literally run to the taxi stand, shout your destination to the driver, and then sit on the edge of your seat hardly able to contain yourself.

By the time you reach your casino-hotel you are *ready* to gamble. "Take my bags upstairs," you instruct the bellman, "I want to check out the casino before I go to my room." And off you go in search of fortunes to be won.

Welcome to the most dangerous hour in casino gambling: your first hour at a casino destination. Many players, unfortunately, will never survive that first 60 minutes. So keyed up to gamble—so hungry for the feast awaiting them at the tables—these individuals will throw caution to the wind, plunging ahead with chips flying, only to end up tapped-out. Totally busted, with no bankroll left, these unfortunate souls have two choices: head back to the airport and catch the next flight home or, worse, sit around the casino for a few days with no gambling funds... the ultimate torture.

When I first started gambling I was a frequent victim of the "first-hour-fiasco" syndrome. There were times I never even saw the inside of the hotel room I had reserved. In fact, before I began practicing the techniques that helped me control myself in the casino, there were times when I actually spent less time gambling than on the cab rides to and from the airport. Certainly not a very enjoyable or profitable way to spend a vacation.

Who Is Most Susceptible To "First-Hour Fiasco"?

Any player has the potential to be caught up in betting fever and fall victim to the most dangerous hour in gambling. The most likely candidates, however, are players who have been away from the casino for an extended period of time, or have to travel a long way to get to the action.

What about you? Are you susceptible to first-hour fiasco? Ask yourself these questions: Do you play differently at the outset of a gambling trip? Are you more reckless? Less controlled? How often do you find yourself hitting the tables before you hit your room? Check with your friends: Do they see a difference in your gaming behavior when you first arrive?

Frankly, I don't believe many players will have trouble determining if they suffer from the dangerous "first-hour" syndrome. The real challenge is to *do* something about it.

The best way to reduce (if not eliminate) the impact of first-hour gambling is, simply, not to gamble for at least one hour after arriving at your casino destination. Further, it is my recommendation that you don't gamble *at all* during your first day at a casino destination, particularly if you've come a long way and are suffering from jet lag. If you must gamble on your arrival day, at least make sure you check into your room first and take a nice, long shower. Get a newspaper, have lunch, go for a walk, shop, do something. *Then* visit the tables when you are refreshed and ready.

It is imperative that you don't concede your psychological edge to the casino in the all-important first hours of your casino stay. **Don't let the hype, the neon, the long trip, or the need for action draw you into the casino before you're psychobiologically ready. Believe me, it's just not worth it.**

Here's a friendly recommendation: The next time you feel the need to gamble immediately after your arrival, try this little exercise. When you're walking from your plane to the baggage claim area, take some time to observe the people preparing to *leave* town. Look at their faces carefully. Note their expressions—the level of energy and optimism in their eyes. Study their posture, their gait, the way they walk as they head to their departure gate. Think about the message all those faces are conveying. Then, once you get to your hotel, go to your room and read this statement over and over:

Every dream has its price. At Disney World, they charge you at the entrance. At the casino, the admission is free... but it costs plenty if you fall victim to the casino's tactics and end up getting taken for a ride.

Take control of that dangerous first-hour at the casino. It'll be 60 minutes well-spent... and your bankroll well-saved.

The Second Most Dangerous Hour In Casino Gambling

If you can make it through the first hour of your casino visit without crashing and burning, you are to be congratulated. But don't pat yourself on the back just yet. You've still need to survive the second most dangerous hour in casino gambling: *the hour before you depart for your trip home*.

In his informative and hard-hitting book, *Casino Gambling Behind the Tables*, my good friend John Alcamo refers to the hour before casino departure as the "getting-even" hour. Players, desperate to recoup their losses, let it all hang out as they pour in fresh reserves of money in a final, frenzied attempt to avoid leaving losers.

Sometimes they succeed.

Most of the times they don't.

The reality of the situation is this: Chasing your losses by betting bigger sums of money is a bad idea... *at any time*. Betting that way with a departure deadline looming makes things even worse. The result? The player is usually overwhelmed by the twin forces of time and monetary pressures, going deeper into—rather than out of—debt.

My recommendation: Don't succumb to the second most dangerous hour in casino gaming. Steel yourself against the temptation of making a final onslaught against the casino just before you depart. Most such attempts end in failure... adding a bitter finale to an already disappointing trip. Be advised: it's almost always a better strategy to "get out of town" with at least some of your bankroll intact rather than throw all your resources into a battle that has already turned against you.

Remember what happened to Custer at Little Bighorn? The casino is no place for a "last stand."

CHAPTER 15

Death Sentence #4:

"Give Me Back The Money I Told You Not To Give Me Back."

You've probably all heard the joke about the gambler who, after experiencing a losing streak, doggedly pursues his spouse out of the casino, yelling: "Give me back the money I told you not to give me back!"

Well, the joke is no laughing matter for the thousands of players who occasionally or habitually lose their financial self-control in the heat of casino action—chasing their losses with funds they had no intention of using. For these individuals, the price of their financial folly can be severe: economic hardship for months, or even years, afterward.

What can players do to *guarantee* they never run the risk of losing more money than they had budgeted for a specific gambling trip? The answer seems simple enough: Don't bring more funds to a gambling destination than you have budgeted to spend. But such a strategy is woefully inadequate in today's computerized credit-card world where ATMs cluster around casino cages like touts at the entrance to a race track.

For players with any type of credit there is only one money protection system that will make it virtually impossible to tap funds not intended for gambling. I know, having developed the approach from earlier "money hunts" on my gambling trips.

Here are the steps you should take if you want to keep yourself from having access to additional funds while on a gambling trip:

1. Take your gambling money with you on the trip, preferably in the form of traveler's checks. Don't plan to get funds once you arrive at your gaming destination.

2. If you have a credit line established at one or more casinos, make sure the total of those credit lines does not exceed the amount of money you have budgeted for your trip. Further, if you have a casino credit line—then do *not* bring out money—otherwise, you run the risk of using both the traveler's checks *and* casino credit—thus, exceeding your budget for the trip. Finally, if you intend to use a casino credit line, make it understood *in writing*, that under no circumstances is the casino permitted to raise your credit limit.

3. Leave at home *all* credit cards, ATM cards, and any other type of instrument such as bank checks, that would allow you to gain access to additional funds.

4. If you *must* take a credit card with you to pay for incidental expenses or to cover you in case of an emergency, make sure the credit line is small, so if you *do* lose control, the damage will be limited.

From a psychological point of view, it is amazing how much better you will gamble when you know you can't get your hands on additional funds. For example, if you have a three-day trip to a casino destination and $3,000 to gamble, you are more likely to budget your funds over the entire three days rather than shooting the whole amount on the first day, if you *know* you can't get a cash advance for additional "ammunition" at any time.

Of course, if you are the kind of player who can go on a three-day gaming trip with a $10,000 credit-line MasterCard in your pocket—lose your allotted $3,000 stake on the first day and *not* tap the credit card for cash— then you won't need this *money-protection system* I'm recommending. You've got enough self-control to make it without safeguards.

But if you find yourself reaching for your checkbook or asking "where can I get a cash advance" even *after* you have lost your budgeted amount for a gambling trip, then maybe you might want to consider taking the steps I recommend. I follow these steps frequently... and they have saved me from financial meltdowns on several occasions.

Sometimes it takes some stringent rules to help boost a person's self-control. Don't be ashamed to give yourself a margin of safety if you feel you need it. It's the kind of protection that makes "cents" (and dollars, too).

Here's a summary of the four *"death sentences"* you don't want to pronounce in the casino.

1. "I didn't come all the way out here to break even."

2. "Wait here a moment while I make a bet to cover our dinner."

3, "Take my bags upstairs—I want to check out the casino before I go to my room."

4. "Give me back the money I told you not to give me back."

SECTION 6

The Eight Gambling Questions Players Ask Me The Most

Fear not to pose a question;
for the inquiring mind
opens the door to success.

H. T. Lockhart

CHAPTER 16

Question #1:

"Should I Go On A Junket?"

Most players really *do* want to beat the casino and come home winners. This is reflected in the questions they ask me... questions that seek to determine if various casino games and promotions are good or bad for the gambler's bankroll. I thought I'd share some of these questions—and my answers—with you. I believe this information will make you a tougher, wiser player, the kind of player casino managers fear the most.

The first question involves the advisability of going on a casino junket. In the 1970s, junkets were a big-time business for the casino industry. In the '80s and early '90s, with the proliferation of casino locations, the junket business declined sharply. However, in the past few years, junket programs have made a comeback in many parts of the country and now provide a gambling option for a significant number of players in the 21st century.

A Junket Is A Casino Comp

In Chapter 3, I discussed *casino comps* under the heading "The free lunch as a last meal." That heading pretty well tells you where *I* stood (and still do) on these casino "freebies": I saw them as another device used by casino operators to seduce the gambler into losing at the tables and slots. When it comes, then, to junkets—the *ultimate* comp—I get *ultimately* concerned about what this might mean for the player's bankroll. In this vein, I am reminded of the junket player who lamented: "I got a free hotel room and ended up paying for the hotel!" A bit of an exaggeration, I'm sure, but still worth thinking about. Yet, with all this said... junkets might be a winning proposition for a *certain kind* of gambler. I'll be discussing what kind of a gambler that is... but first let's take a brief look at what the junket scene is all about.

Junkets: The Ultimate Freebie

In movies, you've made it if you get an Oscar. In science, you're tops if you win the Nobel Prize. And in the world of casino comps, you've reached the pinnacle if you're invited on a "junket."

Not all junkets are the same. Some are better than others, meaning some give away more and better freebies than others. But, basically, if you've got around $10,000 you're willing to put into action at the tables and slots (betting between $25-50 per hand four hours per day), you should be in line for an "RFB" comp: that's free Room, Food, and Beverage for three or four nights at the sponsoring casino-hotel. (Some casinos might also pay your airfare... although the major casino properties would probably require more than $10,000 action to provide this benefit.)

If you don't have that much to risk—say your budget is more like $2,000 to $5,000—then you might end up on a "mini-junket." Mini-junkets are usually one- or two-day trips, often with fewer-frills once you arrive. At the other end of the scale, if you've got a six-figure line ($100,000 and up) to play with, things can really get interesting: first-class airfare, the privilege of bringing along a guest for free, a palatial suite at the sponsoring hotel, gourmet everything, free shows, use of a free limo, and even "cash-back" incentives based on your gambling handle.

At this point I'd like to clarify an issue that often creates confusion when people talk about junkets. When a casino requires, say, $10,000 for a front-money deposit or credit line in order for you to attend a junket, it is *not* requiring you to lose the $10,000. The casino is only asking that you be willing to *risk that amount of money in action at the tables or slots*. Whether you win or lose really makes no difference to them. The casino operators play the percentages: They know a certain proportion of monies gambled will, in the long run, end up in their hands. A casino executive might put it this way to the player: "We're willing to spend some money on you, if you're willing to give us a reasonable shot at your bank-roll."

Can anyone really deny that such a request is reasonable?

Getting The Best Junket Bargain

If you do decide to go the junket route, you might as well get the most value for your action. Here are some suggestions to help you achieve that objective.

1. **Shop around for the best junket deal.** The rapid expansion of casinos throughout the world has created a "buyer's market" of sorts. Competition for premium players is intense, and that means better bargains for those willing to look for them. Therefore, it pays to comparison shop *before* you select a junket destination. Your goal is to locate the junket that offers the best comps for the level of money you're willing to put into action.

   As an example, I know of one junket program that offers the $10,000 player an RFB comp, plus $500 in complimentary casino chips. Other junket programs require the same $10,000 front money, but do not offer the $500 in chips. Let's face it, an extra $500 can sometimes make the difference between a winning and losing trip to the casino.

2. **Watch for special promotions or events.** Many casinos have special occasions involving attractive inducements for players. These events usually occur during slack visiting times, and if you have a flexible travel schedule you can take advantage of these programs.

3. **Try to find junkets that require the least sizable bet or spread of bets to warrant specific comps.** As an example, two casinos might offer the same

RFB comp for a $10,000 bettor. Yet, one establishment might require $50 minimum bets and $100 spread action on the dice table; while another casino might only require $25 minimum bets and $50 spread action at craps.

4. **Try to find junkets that require the least playing time to qualify for the comps in question.** To illustrate, one casino might require the gambler to play five hours a day to receive airfare and an RFB comp; while another establishment, offering the same incentives, might only require four playing hours a day.

5. **Play only at those establishments that provide good "PAIR": Payoffs, Atmosphere, Interaction, and Rules, as we learned in Chapter 4.** Don't accept casino comps—no matter how attractive—if the price of such freebies is gambling in a casino where you'll have a more difficult time of winning.

6. **In considering the value of the junket package you are receiving, don't forget to factor in the quality of the hotel-casino where you will be staying.** If two hotel-casinos offer you the same junket package but one establishment is a "four star" accommodation and the other a "run of the mill" property, then the junket packages aren't really equal, are they?

7. **You might want to consider setting up a "splinter junket" directly with the casino.** This kind of individualized junket gives you far greater flexibility in arriving and leaving your casino destination. I used to set up my own junkets quite frequently when I

was into the junket scene. It gave me more opportunity to be by myself and, most important, allowed me to begin and end my trip whenever I wanted. Being able to end a casino visit on the spur of the moment (not having to wait till the end of a regularly scheduled junket) can often mean the difference between winning and losing at the tables. This little drama is played out far too often: A member of an organized gambling junket makes a big killing his or her first day at the casino, only to lose all of it back while waiting for the junket to end.

Should You Go On A Junket?

Some people argue—and it is a good argument—that if you're going to gamble big anyway, you might as well let the casino pay your expenses. But there are potential problems with junkets, and these problems center on the psychological side of individual gamblers. In my three decades of gaming experience as both a player and behavioral scientist, it has become evident that some players have the proper frame of mind for successful junket participation, and others do not.

What kind of player are you? Do you have the proper disposition to go on a junket... and not end up junked? To answer this question, let's examine the behavior of three individuals who accepted junket offers to a hotel-casino in Las Vegas. Although they are fictional characters, each of these "Three Junketeers" represents a personality "type" frequently encountered on freebie gambling trips.

The First Junketeer was **Larson Ness.** He had been gambling for years and figured he could beat the casinos out of a five-day vacation. When he got to Las Vegas he deposited his check in the cage and promptly shuttled his way between the pool and the gourmet restaurant.

When he finally did get around to gambling, he would draw out a marker and then table hop—trying to confuse casino management as to the length of his play and size of his action.

In fact, Larson never fooled anybody. Casino personnel are highly trained to spot freeloaders, and do so with a remarkable degree of speed and accuracy. If you're planning to go on a junket with an eye to fooling the casino into a risk-free vacation, forget it. Chances are you'll be caught—with uncomfortable consequences for all concerned. Players who don't hold up their end of the junket commitment by putting their bankroll in action are often asked to pay for the bills that would have been comped. If the casino is "nice about it" you might simply be written off as a deadbeat... a downside risk of doing junket business. Don't, however, expect to receive *any* future junket invitations.

The Second Junketeer was **E. Z. Mark**, a player who couldn't wait to experience all the freebies that awaited him. When he hit Vegas, he plunged into his comps with a vengeance—eating and drinking like there was no tomorrow. The casino personnel treated him regally, too. They called him "Mr. M" at the tables and lavished special attention on him at poolside and in the showroom. He didn't even have to stand in lines. Mr. Mark became "Mr. Invited Guest" for the length of his stay.

Unfortunately, all this spectacular treatment affected E. Z.'s gambling behavior in a negative manner. Whereas in the past he had been a relatively well-controlled, disciplined player, now he seemed bent on creating a high-rolling image at the tables. He bet more money, bet it recklessly, and began tipping outlandishly. "After all," he thought, "I'm being treated like royalty, so I better start betting accordingly."

Furthermore, when he did win any money he felt vaguely guilty, like a person taking money from a close friend. It's not surprising, then, that by the end of the trip E. Z. had bet away his front money.

The Third Junketeer was **Seymour Profitt**. Like E. Z. Mark, he was an experienced casino gambler. Unlike E. Z., he was aware of the seductive qualities of "free lunches." When he arrived at the casino he was impressed by the quality and extent of the treatment afforded him, but he did not let it affect his gambling judgment or behavior. When he won, he didn't feel guilty. When he lost, he didn't feel relieved. When people treated him like royalty, he refrained from wagering his kingdom. When the casino personnel rated his action he didn't try to show off, but wagered as he always did: at reasonable levels that still fulfilled the casino's time and wagering requirements. And finally, when he calculated his gaming stake he didn't say "I can afford to lose $1,000 because that's how much expense money I'm saving on this junket."

There you have the Three Junketeers. Recognize yourself? Can you remain unseduced and guiltless in the face of casino favors? Can you keep your gambling in bounds when you're supposed to be a premium player and the casino is checking out your action? Most important: Will you bet the same way on a junket as you would normally? If you can, then maybe junkets are for you.

Want to know what I do? I seldom go on junkets anymore. Why? Because I agree with casino executive Barney Vinson, author of *Las Vegas Behind The Tables*, when he says: "There are a lot of things that are free in Las Vegas, but son, you can't afford them." And that, dear reader, says it all!

CHAPTER 17

Question #2:

"Can Money Management Help Me In The Casino?"

Yes.

A system of money management will allow you to utilize your financial resources in a manner that maximizes your chances for profit and minimizes your chances for loss. Before I present the principles of effective money management let me tell you about a middle-aged lady by the name of Carolyn.

I first met Carolyn playing the slots. Perfectly dressed and manicured, she looked every inch the conservative Boston banker... until she hit a minor jackpot. At that moment the image of conservatism went out the window, as she began shouting and wagering with the zeal of a high roller from Texas.

I watched her play for about ten minutes. She didn't hit another jackpot but she kept betting like The Last Desperado... and I wondered how long her winnings would hold out.

Not long. About half an hour later she wandered into the coffee shop where I was eating, and waved hello.

"How'd you make out?" I asked, already certain of her answer.

She rolled her eyes. "Wiped out. Not a thing left."

"Maybe you should've left when the machine cooled off," I suggested, hoping Carolyn wouldn't be offended by my unsolicited advice.

"Perhaps..." she responded, thoughtfully. "Seems I never know when to quit."

I decided to press my recommendation further. "Have you ever thought about setting loss limits at the slots?" I paused, studying Carolyn's expression for several moments. "Have you ever practiced money management?"

Carolyn nodded affirmatively. "Sure I practice money management. I play until my money runs out."

As you might guess, money management experts aren't overly impressed with Carolyn's system. Some of their systems, however, are not much better. Many are too complex to understand. Others reduce the excitement of gambling to an exercise in boredom, leaving one to wonder if there is life after money management in the casino.

Actually, sound money management needn't be unintelligible or boring. It *can* be beneficial... but before I show you why, let me first tell you what money management *cannot* do.

In the long run, no money management system ever created can turn a negative-expectation wager into a positive expectation of profit for the player. Martingale... Great Martingale... Ponzer... D'lambert; no matter what the system, if the percentages are against you, you will eventually lose.

I'm sending you a sobering message: If we play baccarat, roulette, craps—or any other casino game where the house has the percentage in its favor—we are going to end up losing in the long run, *regardless* of the system we use.

But note the key phrase "*...in the long run.*" It is true that if we wagered an infinite amount of money over an infinite number of trials, we would end up losing a percentage of our stake that was equal to the house edge in that particular game. But what about the short run? After all, we are not immortal, nor do we possess unlimited wealth; thus, none of us will be wagering from a bottomless bankroll through an eternity of casino visits. In the short run, money management *can* make a difference. It is here—during individual gambling sessions or trips—that money management can have an impact on how quickly and how much we win or lose.

Let me show you how. Assume you have $1,000 to gamble at craps during a one-hour session. Assume further that you bet only the pass-line, where the house edge is 1.41 percent. You decide to go with a Martingale double-up money management system. You start with a $1 bet on the line. If you win, you pocket your profit and bet $1 again. If you lose, you double your bet—and keep doubling until you win, hit the house limit or go bust. Here's what happens. You win your first three bets. On your fourth wager, however, you lose... and keep losing. Your wagers look like this: $1, $2, $4, $8, $16, $32, $64, $128, $256, $512, $1,024. In eleven wagers you would have lost more than your *entire* $1,000 stake!

Now, let us pretend that instead of the Martingale system you had decided to go with a "flat" bet money management wagering system: betting $1 at a time on the pass-line, win or lose. After an hour of play at a moderately busy crap table it would be *highly* unusual if you were winning or losing more than $25. It would be impossible to lose even close to $100... let alone the $1,000 lost betting the Martingale system.

Note what happened: By using the flat wagering system, we eliminate the possibility of going broke in an hour. With the Martingale system, on the other hand, the chance for losing our entire bankroll is *always* there. Thus, we see that money management wagering systems can— and do—affect how much and how quickly we win or lose. And it is the wagering system's ability to regulate these two factors—in the short run—that makes money management betting systems a relevant gaming tool.

A Money Management System For Negative-Expectation Games

What kind of money management strategy is best for *you?* In Chapter 2, we pointed out that if you want the best possible chance of making a profit, then you should make one bet with your total bankroll. If you want the longest possible time to play at the tables, you should break your bankroll into as many bets as possible.

Obviously, *your* optimal money management strategy will be determined, then, by what *you* want out of gambling: more time at the tables or more money in your pocket. Most likely, a middle-ground strategy would be appropriate for most players. Such a strategy won't give you the best chance of winning, nor will it give you the best chance of staying the longest possible time at the tables. What it *will* give you is a reasonable chance of winning in the short run with a reasonable amount of playing time.

In using this "middle ground" strategy, *bet sizing* becomes very important.

How large should your wagers be? They should be large enough to make them interesting, yet give you a chance for a meaningful win. They should be small enough to provide meaningful playing time at the tables and allow you to weather most runs of adverse results should they occur.

This betting approach is in keeping with a money management strategy in which we are not betting for maximum profits or maximum time at the tables, but, rather, for a reasonable chance of winning with a reasonable amount of playing time.

I am going to recommend that your original wager for a gambling session be between 2 and 3 percent of your allotted bankroll for that session. Thus, if you have a $100 stake for a particular session, the size of your starting wager should be in the $2-$3 range. Should you begin winning at the table, you may choose to raise your bets as your bankroll increases, but the percentage of the bet in proportion to your bankroll size should stay pretty much in the 2 to 3 percent range.

Thus, if your $100 bankroll balloons to $200, then you could wager between $4 and $6. You may also choose to decrease your bet if your initial bankroll shrinks. Again, this is optional, but not a bad idea.

My bet-sizing recommendations should be viewed as general guidelines, not fixed rules. In the final analysis, you should bet an amount that feels most comfortable for you, within the boundaries of the available money you have to spend and in keeping with your reasons for gambling in the first place. If you want to bet higher than the 2 to 3 percent figure I have suggested, this is your call, but you should realize that your chances of being wiped out increase along with your opportunities for greater profit.

Money Management Strategy
For Playing Positive-Expectation Games

Up to this point, we have been discussing the use of money management in casino games where you have the worst of it; where the house has a mathematical advantage in its favor.

But what about casino games and activities that can be beaten through skillful play, such as poker, blackjack, some progressive slots, and race and sports wagering? It is here that money management strategy is different.

In any game or activity where you have the odds in *your* favor, you will win... in the *long* run. In this sense you are no different from the casino with its positive expectation over gamblers at the craps and baccarat tables. Note again, however, the critical importance of the words *"in the long run."* In the *short run*—even with the odds in your favor—you *can* (and will) suffer losses. Ask any skillful blackjack or poker player who has faced a run of bad cards and he or she will vouch for the validity of short-run loss.

So what should you do? Why not take a hint from the casinos? Gaming establishment operators are savvy business people. They recognize that the house can suffer short-term losing streaks, even with the odds in its favor. To guard against financial ruin during these times, casinos set betting limits at the tables. This "house limit" protects the casino bankroll against a lucky assault by a hot gambler. You should do the same. **When the long-term odds of winning are in your favor, your money management goal should be to protect your bankroll from destruction during short-term losing streaks.**

This can be done by dividing your bankroll into a number of wagers sufficient to weather a string of short-term losses. Of course, as you win and your bankroll grows, the chances of being wiped out by a short-term losing streak decrease, assuming the size of your bets remain the same. Therefore, it is appropriate to increase the size of your bets as your total gaming stake expands, but never so quickly as to jeopardize your total bankroll.

Special Circumstances

I have just described a basic money management strategy for use when the odds are in *your* favor. In general, it will serve you well. Of course, there are individual circumstances when a deviation from the strategy is not only appropriate, but required. One case in point might be in a no-limit hold-'em game where your total gambling bankroll is on the table in front of you and you have "the nuts" (an unbeatable hand). If you think you will get a call from your opponent, it is perfectly reasonable that you would go all in—even though you are wagering your entire bankroll on one bet. The reason for deviating from basic money management strategy in this case is that you can't lose, and you want to get maximum benefit from your hand.

A Final Word

Money management is neither a panacea nor a waste of time. It is a gambling *tool* and, when used skillfully, it can help the player bet more effectively in the casino. When playing games with the odds in your favor, you can use money management to protect your bankroll while seeking financial gain. When faced with contests where the house has the edge, you can employ money management to strike an appropriate balance between making a short-term profit and staying in action at the tables. All in all, I concur with the comment of baccarat player Sue Hirsch who observed: "I manage my money because that's the only way I can manage to win."

CHAPTER 18

Question #3:

"Should I Gamble In Casinos Outside The United States?"

Here's something to think about: You're on vacation with your husband in fabled Monte Carlo, and here you are winning wager after wager at the roulette table. People press in around you, reaching out to touch you... to capture some of your good fortune. An elegant gentleman with exquisitely blue eyes and a dazzling smile leans over and whispers something French into your ear. You nod knowingly and wait for the croupier to start the ivory ball on its way to your winning number. "One moment please," the voice belongs to the casino manager, who has approached your table and now is speaking directly to you. "I am sorry, Madam," he says in perfect English, "but we will have to close this table. You have broken the bank."

Perhaps you like this scenario even better: You're in a posh London casino, playing Chemmy. The shoe passes to you. Across the table a sneering, heavyset man places a thousand pounds on player and dares you to match his bet. You do... and you win. The punter challenges you again and doubles his bet. You win again. The punter goes the house limit and gives you a twisted smile. You stay with him... and win again. You hold the shoe for 15 coups, winning a fortune and reducing your adversary to a whimpering, broken man.

Breaking the bank at Monte Carlo. Winning at the baccarat table James Bond-style in London. Such fantasies are standard fare for the gambler. It is no secret that most of us daydream of gambling on foreign shores... in casinos strange and exotic. Nor are such dreams necessarily bad. But, if you actually attempt to visit a foreign casino to turn your fantasy into reality—be careful. Your dream could become a nightmare if you don't take some important preliminary steps before leaving the familiar gambling confines of the U.S.A. Here are some things to keep in mind *before* you pack your bags and set off in quest of fortune:

Learn About The Casinos
You Will Be Visiting

If you were going to set up a business in a foreign land, I am sure you would find out all you could about the country and its customs before putting up your money. Why should doing business with a foreign casino be any different? It is crucial that you learn all you can about the casinos you intend to visit... particularly when you consider that although there are differences between casinos in America, these differences are minor compared to the differences you will encounter between American casinos and some foreign gaming establishments.

Some of my most unpleasant playing experiences could have been easily avoided had I taken the time to check out foreign casinos before visiting them. For example, when I first went on a gambling trip to the Bahamas, I failed to check out the rules and payoffs for craps. I paid dearly for this mistake. When I arrived, I found that the casino dealt "Eastern style" craps, where no come-bets are allowed. This is a very unfavorable game for the player and I ended up having to play other casino games when I really wanted to have a go at the dice tables. But, at least I got to gamble.

A year later when I went to England for my first go at the London clubs, I discovered I had to wait 48 hours to play at all. And, seeing that I only had a 24-hour layover in London, that meant I missed out on gambling altogether. Such are the kinds and magnitudes of disappointment awaiting the gambler who doesn't do his or her homework.

What You'll Want To Know About Foreign Casinos

Before heading off to exotic lands to wager your francs or pounds, do take time to find out the following information:

1. the kinds of games available

2. the rules of play governing games that interest you

3. the payoffs for various wagers

4. betting limits and restrictions

5. credit policies (if you are a credit player)

6. dress requirements (if any)

7. food and drink policies (if it makes a difference to you)

8. tipping customs/procedures (in some casinos it is not allowed... in other establishments the employees will help themselves to some of your winning chips if you're not careful!)

9. language spoken (believe me, being able to speak French can make a difference when disputes over chip ownership erupt at a French roulette table)

10. casino entry fees (if any)

11. "waiting periods" before one can gamble (if any)

12. currency procedures (exchange rates, type utilized for gaming, rules for bringing cash into and out of the host country)

13. comps available (what types, how much action required to get them)

14. security procedures (availability of safety deposit boxes and security personnel; degree of safety should you decide to transport your winnings from the casino to another destination)

Should You Play In A
"Floating" Craps Game?

What about gambling aboard a cruise ship? It sounds romantic and exciting. In fact, it *is* romantic and exciting. Imagine your own floating hotel, complete with private state room, frequent, lavish meals, first-run movies, variety shows, swimming pool, casino, and disco—even bingo, skeet shooting, and stopovers in exotic ports. And don't forget the moonlit nights as you take a midnight stroll in the sea-fresh air. Most cruise ships offer these amenities for as little as $100-200 a day, per person, which isn't that much when you consider that room and board are included in the price.

If you think you'd like the idea of a gambling cruise, then by all means... pack up and hit the high seas (Let's make that *calm* seas!). But do a little homework first. Finding out about shipboard gaming is absolutely critical... maybe even more so than with land-based casinos. This is because with land-based casinos you can pack up and walk away if you don't like what's being offered. That's not possible when you're on a ship. You're pretty much stuck for the duration of the cruise... and that can be pretty nasty if you don't like what's being offered in the shipboard casino.

When investigating shipboard casinos, follow the same 14-point checklist I've provided for land-based gaming establishments. Be sure to get accurate answers to the following questions:

1. **"Is there a casino aboard the cruise ship?"** A growing number of cruise ships are including casino gam-

bling among their shipboard activities; yet there are casino-less ships. Check directly with the cruise line on this one.

2. **"What games are included?"** Very few ships have "full-service" casinos.

3. **"What are the payouts and rules of play?"** Be aware that on most cruise ships the odds and rules offered the player are not as favorable as those offered in many land-based establishments. The reason is obvious: Unless you walk on water, it is difficult to leave your shipboard casino for another establishment with more player-favorable policies.

4. **"What are the hours of operation?"** Very few shipboard casinos are operational 24 hours a day.

5. **"What are the betting limits?"** They are generally *very* restrictive when compared with land-based casinos. Sometimes limits are raised for players if they have arranged this with the cruise line *in advance* of the sailing date.

6. **"What are the credit policies?"** *Dollars float, but people don't.* That bit of wisdom suggests it is more difficult to get cash aboard a ship than on land. Therefore, if you anticipate a potential "cash crunch," you should find out if you can: (a) get cash advances from your credit-debit cards; (b) cash traveler's checks for play at the tables; and (c) play off your markers... and settle up later.

Gambling aboard most cruise ships provides a satisfying blend of casino action with the intimate friendliness of the neighborhood poker game. The lower wagering limits and easygoing shipboard rhythms add to this sense of congeniality. So does the "cozy" size of most shipboard casinos and the generally friendly casino staff. Of course, as with any gambling games, you can lose... and if you run out of money aboard a seagoing vessel, it isn't easy to make an unscheduled return home. So play smart, manage your money carefully and accept my best wishes for *Victory at Sea*.

Some Final Recommendations
For Gambling In Casinos
Outside The United States

Gambling in a foreign country (or on the high seas) can be exciting and memorable. Don't let down your guard, however. Whenever you are in a casino—at home or "away"—your major purpose is to win. If you want to keep your psychobiological edge in foreign casinos, you must remember that no matter how exotic or different the establishment is—no matter how much entertainment you experience during play—you are still there to beat the house. In that spirit, I make these final observations and wish you bon voyage:

1. Gamble only in legal casinos that are well-established and have a reputation for honesty and fair play.

2. Be sure of the local rules and casino conditions *before* you play... and be sure to follow all customs or rules in the foreign countries you visit.

3. Gamble only in those establishments where your chances of winning are as good as in the American casino(s) of your choice. If you can't find such an establishment where you are (or where you intend to travel), then save your gambling for other destinations where the chances of winning are better. It will save you money *and* peace of mind in the long run.

CHAPTER 19

Question #4

"Is It Possible To Beat the Slots?"

In the 1970s, when I first started gambling in casinos, the only way you could beat the slots was with your fists or, preferably, a sledgehammer. The "one-armed bandit" label for those voracious machines was truly well-deserved.

How things have changed! Today, you can play the slots without ever pulling their "arms" and you *can* beat them if you are either: (a) *very, very* lucky or (b) *very, very* skilled.

Beat the slots!? Can this truly be possible? Yes, but don't sell the homestead in search of unlimited riches. Winning at slots might well be the most difficult way to make money yet devised by the human race. And it all became possible with the introduction of the *progressive jackpot*. The progressive jackpot gives the slot player two ways to win:

1. **The lucky way.** With the introduction of linked jackpot machines like *Megabucks, Cool Millions,* and *Quartermania,* the player can literally win *millions*

of dollars on an investment of a few bucks. Playing these machines is much like playing the lottery: your chances of winning are *very* slim... but if you *do* win, then you will probably end up a winner over time. Why? Well, it is unlikely that someone who wins millions of dollars on a slot or in the lottery will gamble back enough of it to let the negative-expectation aspects of the game take their toll.

The problem with playing this type of machine, of course, is that the winner's profit must come from somewhere. That "somewhere" is all the losing bets made by the thousands upon thousands of players who are wagering for the same jackpot but never get it. What this means is that if you play these lottery-type slots, your chances of winning are *infinitesimally* small. Even with the smaller payouts available on such machines, your chances of walking away ahead after, say, an hour of play, are very poor. Thus, the only realistic reason for playing this type of machine is for the thrill of "going for the big one." And it is for that reason that I recommend very limited amounts of money be wagered on such machines. Such gambling must be viewed as entertainment only, because the chances of winning are so remote that to play them for profit would fly in the face of every recommended strategy in this book.

2. **The skillful way.** The convergence of two innovations in slots—*progressive jackpots* and *video poker*—has provided the skilled player the opportunity to *beat* the slots in the long run. This is because, for the first time in slot history, a machine has been created with

rules and payouts offering a *positive-expectation* for the player.

Why does the player have to be *skilled* to win on such machines? Because without expert play (knowing how to play each hand correctly and knowing how large the jackpot must be to justify play), the gambler's mathematical edge disappears and the edge swings to the house side. In this sense, expert play at slots is exactly like expert play at blackjack: Players who cannot count cards and recognize favorable rules of play surrender *their* edge to the house and become mathematically favored to lose rather than win.

If you want to become a video poker expert and take a shot at beating the machines, I wish you good skill! Read *Video Poker Mania,* by Dwight and Louise Crevelt for professional advice on beating what has become the casino's hottest slot. They give you the strategies necessary to accomplish such a feat, but first, let *me* tell you that (1) it will *not* be easy; (2) finding machines with the proper-sized jackpot to justify play will be a challenge (many machines are hit before the jackpot gets to the necessary level... and those machines with a sufficiently high jackpot are often crowded with people waiting to play them); and (3) ultimate winnings depend on your getting your statistical "fair share" of jackpot hands (royal flushes). Because a royal flush normally occurs only once every 40,000 hands on average, you can see your bankroll might suffer significant shrinkage waiting for a progressive jackpot to hit.

Personally, I have yet to meet a player who is ahead in the long run on the progressive jackpot video poker machines. For that reason, I would not get real excited about winning big and consistently on these slots. If you learn to play them properly you can take satisfaction in knowing that such machines present you with the lowest casino edge on any slot currently in service and, possibly, with patience, skill, and the ability to find the properly sized jackpots, you might actually be able to swing the odds in your favor and win in the long run.

For Those Of You Who Don't Plan To Become Video Poker Pros

Many of you reading this book want to—and will—play the slots but don't intend to put in the time and effort necessary to attempt winning play at the progressive video poker machines. Is there a way to maximize *your* chances of winning in the short run and reduce the size of your losses in the long run? Yes. I'll show you that way in a moment. Remember, however, that like all negative-expectation games in the casino, slots sporting a house edge *will be* losers for you over an extended period of play.

Getting A Handle On The Bandit

What does a bowl of potato chips and a bowl of quarters have in common? If you're one of the millions of people who enjoy playing slot machines, you know the answer: You keep reaching for one more! And therein lies one of the major reasons that slot revenues continue to enrich casino coffers at record rates. People don't seem able to walk away from one-armed bandits until their total playing bankroll has been exhausted.

Even more surprising are gamblers who regularly practice "stop loss" and "winning bet lockup" methods at table games, but seem unable or unwilling to do the same when it comes to money management at the slots.

Money Management:
The Key To Slot Survival

I learned the importance of slot money management the hard way—as a victimized player.

The scenario was always the same. I would go to the change booth, get some rolls of coins, and then select a machine. Then the carnage began. I would insert my original investment of coins. Feed and pull. Feed and pull. When those coins ran out, I would reach into the bowl for any payouts. Feed and pull. Feed and pull. I would lunge into the bowl again and again—like the compulsive potato chip addict—until there were no coins left, until the infernal machine had gobbled up everything I had. Only then did the compulsive "feeding behavior" stop, allowing me to stagger away from the machine to lick my financial wounds and contemplate the folly of my gambling frenzy.

It became painfully apparent that the only way I could avoid financial oblivion in Slot Land was to develop a system that protected my machine payouts and kept them off-limits for reinvestment into the machine. The approach I developed is simple to use and it works, *but it must be followed without exception*. To deviate from the strategy is to court certain disaster.

Your Strategy

In all casino games, you need to make three decisions:
(1) How much you are willing to win; (2) how much you
are willing to lose; and (3) how long you want to play.

In slot machine gambling, where the percentages almost always favor the house, you need to recognize that
the longer you play, the greater the likelihood you will
suffer financial loss. On the other hand, a certain amount
of play will be required if you are to satisfy your "need
for action."

Here is my money management strategy for extending
your playing time while giving you a gambling chance to
bring some winnings home.

1. Decide how many slot gaming sessions you want per
    trip. Using my money management recommendations,
    the average session will take 15–30 minutes to com-
    plete, which includes procurement of gaming tokens,
    choosing a machine, playing the coins, and cashing
    in.

2. Decide on the denomination(s) of slots you wish to
    play—quarter, dollar, etc.

3. Start each gaming session with enough tokens to play
    20-50 times based on depositing the maximum num-
    ber of coins playable on your chosen machine. Ex-
    ample: On a three-coin dollar progressive, you would
    need $99 to get 33 plays in the session. **It is particu-
    larly important to play the maximum number of
    coins allowed if you are on a jackpot machine—as
    this is the only way you can win the jackpot.**

4. Purchase the total amount of coins/tokens you intend to play for the session. *Do not use the machine's bill acceptor or play credits as this eliminates the opportunity to use my money management system.*

5. Choose the machine you want to play. I recommend that you play only one machine per session. Playing one machine helps you avoid the temptation of mixing your original playing stake with machine payouts as you move from machine to machine. Also, keeping your pulls to a 50-maximum protects you against playing a "tight" machine too long.

6. Put your playing stake (all the coins or tokens you purchased) in a cup. Take coins from that cup to insert in the machine. Under *no* circumstances should you place any of your playing stake in the payout bowl. It is imperative that you keep your playing stake separate from any payouts from the machine.

7. Commence play. If you hit winners, let the machine-paid coins accumulate in the payout bowl. *Never, never touch the paid-out coins while play is in progress. They must remain in the payout bowl until the session ends.*

8. End the session whenever you feel you want to, or when you have exhausted your playing stake, whichever comes first.

9. At the end of the session remove any machine payouts that have accumulated in the bowl. *Do not—under any condition—reinsert these coins into any slot*

machine. Bring these coins directly to the change booth and cash out. Then take a break.

10. When you are ready to begin your next session with the slots, repeat the 9-point strategy all over again.

11. Once you have completed the number of slot sessions you scheduled for your trip, do *not* gamble again. This is a rule that must be followed regardless of your financial standing at the time. Winner or loser—it is time to call it quits. That's what money management is all about.

A Few Playing Options

Here are a few modifications you can make to my slot machine money management system. Use them only if you think they are more appropriate for your style of play.

1. If at anytime during a session you should win a jackpot that is at least *50 times* the value of the coins you put in *for that pull only*, take that jackpot amount out of the tray, lock it up, and never play it again on the trip. (Example: On a given pull, you put in three dollars and hit a jackpot of $150, this is 50 times your investment and should be "locked up." If you can, buy a postal money order and send this money home so it will be waiting for you when you return.

2. f you have completed a particular session (you have played through your entire playing stake) but don't want to leave the machine because it is *hot,* do this:

Count up the amount of coins in the payout bowl. If the amount is at least *twice* your original playing stake (you doubled your money), lock up your initial stake and play through the remaining amount... *once only!* If the amount in the payout bowl is not twice your original stake, then take what is in there and get away from the machine! It's not "hot" enough to justify further play.

Here are a few more ideas for getting the most out of your slot dollars:

1. **Shop around for bargains.** Competition for the gambling dollar has created a player's market for slots... but you've got to comparison shop to get the best deals. Video poker machines are the only slots where you can actually determine the best values. Compare the payout tables (e.g., some machines pay on 10s or better; others offer 6-9 rather than 5-8 payouts). On the reel-type slots, there's really no way to know what the casino edge is. This is because each machine can be programmed to give the house whatever edge it desires (within legal limits). Recently, however, this has changed with the introduction of "carousels," a specific circle (or bank) of dollar slots with larger payouts and lower house advantages. The casino edge, usually 2 to 4 percent, is clearly posted for the gambler to see. The "carousels" are a definite improvement from the slot player's point of view. The percentage is usually lower than on other machines throughout the casino. Yet, one must keep in mind the larger bankroll (and investment) necessary

to get this lower house advantage. In general, the house edge is greatest for the nickel, dime, and quarter slots and smallest for the large denomination machines.

2. **If there is a "slot club" in the casino where you play, become a member.** Membership is free and entitles you to a wide variety of benefits, including cash back for your play. Because the slots pay out the same amount whether you are a member of the slot club or not, it is foolish to miss out on membership benefits. Earning slot "points" is like earning frequent flier miles when you fly. It's a good deal.

    There are only two potential drawbacks to slot clubs: (a) Some casinos that save costs by *not* having slot clubs advertise better payouts on their machines. Serious slot players would be advised to consider this in their choice of playing locations. (b) Some slot clubs have "countdowns" on their machines to earn credit points. Don't let these countdown numbers influence your commitment to end play when your buy-in stake has been wagered. I shudder when I see gamblers take "a few coins out of the bowl" just to complete the countdown... and end up losing every coin left in their payout bowl. If you start playing for slot club points rather than to win at the slots, then don't become a member of the club. It's not worth it.

3. **Know your machine.** Read all machine instructions carefully. Understand how payouts are made and how

you can qualify for them. If you have any questions, ask a casino official before you begin to play.

4. **Check your payoffs.** Don't assume your machine is perfect. After all, if a vending machine can short-change you, so can a slot. Check your first two pay-offs for any discrepancies. If you discover an under-payment, report it to the casino so you can be reimbursed. If you discover an overpayment... please save the machine and write me in care of the publisher!

A Final Word

Except for *highly* skilled play at certain kinds of progressive video poker (and the occasional 10-million-to-one winner on the "lottery" slots), there really is no way to beat the one-armed bandits in the long run. Because almost all slots carry a house edge greater than 1.6 percent, I don't recommend them for play. If you *must* have a go at them, at least don't wager too much money and follow the strategies I recommend. That way you won't get seriously burned. Good luck... and may you win many jackpots.

I'll be *pulling* for you.

CHAPTER 20

Question #5:

"Should I Play In Casino Tournaments?"

Some children grow up wanting to be firemen. Others desire a career in law or medicine. Me? I grew up wanting to be a sports champion. Unfortunately, my body didn't get the message. And now a cursory glance in my direction will reveal a body at war with middle age, with middle age definitely winning.

In fact, the only hint of athletic prowess in my otherwise spreading physique is the "stooping posture" characteristic in those of us who spend significant hours hunched over crowded craps tables.

Yet, even though I've always been short on physical ability, the lust for competition still coursed through my veins. The problem was: How could I satisfy my longings to take the playing field and win?

The answer to my question came quite unexpectedly in 1981, via an invitation to participate in a most unusual sporting event, one that would crown a world champion at the end of the competition.

And there was more. Not only would one competitor emerge a world champion, he or she would also be awarded a cash prize of $65,000! Best of all, the competition was perfectly suited to my unique athletic skills and background—it was a *dice competition*, the World Championship of Craps, to be held at the Riviera Hotel in Las Vegas.

I can still recall the feeling of exhilaration that enveloped me as I faced my craps-shooting opponents across the green felt... the smooth red dice cocked smartly in my right hand, a rack full of chips stacked neatly near my left hand, a look of supreme confidence on my face.

I can still remember the shouting and pleading that filled the crowded casino as 1,006 cigar-toting, Texas-style craps-shooters exhorted the dice to go their way.

And I can still recollect the anticipated thrill of victory and, alas, the ultimate agony of defeat, as the championship crown eluded me. Even though I was one of five players to win first place in the team event, I did not prevail in the singles competition, and watched in silent despair as the world title was bestowed on Ken Meserve, Jr., a tax advisor from San Jose, California.

Casino Tournaments Come Of Age

Although it wasn't my destiny to become the first World Champion of Craps, it was my good fortune to be a part of gaming history. As it turned out, the Riviera championship—labeled by one local newspaper as "the best casino promotion in Las Vegas history"—was the catalyst that vaulted casino tournaments to the forefront of gaming activity and player popularity.

The World Championship of Craps was certainly not the first casino tournament (Binion's World Series of Poker, for example, was already 12 years old in 1981), nor was it the richest. But its potential, in terms of popularity and applicability to all casino games, made it an idea whose time had come.

Today, there are tournaments to fit the taste and budgets of almost every casino player. There are tournaments for baccarat, slots, blackjack, dice, roulette... even keno and sports handicapping. There are tournaments developed, sponsored, and hosted by individual casinos. And there are tournaments developed and hosted by independent operators (although these have almost disappeared from the contemporary casino scene). There are "professional" tournaments and "amateur" tournaments; satellite tournaments and celebrity tournaments; tournaments with entry fees of $10,000 and tournaments with entry fees of $22. There are tournaments played on an annual basis and tournaments played on a one-time basis. There are tournaments that last an hour, others that last a week or more. There are tournaments played on the high seas and tournaments played in the High Sierras.

All of which means that if you want to experience the excitement, camaraderie, and possible financial benefits of a casino tournament, the opportunity has never been better. In fact, it is currently a "buyer's market," with special bargains available to the discriminating player who takes the time to shop around for the best deals.

Why Do Casinos Host Gaming Tournaments?

As we have already learned in the third chapter of this book, casinos are in business to make money—*your money*—and the job of casino executives is to develop and market gaming activities that will lead to greater profits. Casino gaming tournaments are no exception to this general rule. If the casino operators did not see these events as money-makers, they would not sponsor or conduct them.

Does this mean, then, that you, the player, must necessarily lose money when you enter a tournament? No. In fact, there are times when your chances of winning money in a tournament are better than your chances of winning money playing at the tables in non-tournament action. The reason for this apparent paradox is that sometimes casinos will run tournaments that actually lose money to the players, with the hope that they will recoup their losses and turn an eventual profit in the long run because of tournament-generated customer loyalty and non-tournament play.

Here, then, are some of the reasons casinos are involved in the tournament gaming business:

1. To introduce players to the casino, and encourage them to play there in the future. It is assumed that a player who forms a positive impression of the casino during a tournament will choose to gamble there again in the future, in *non*-tournament play.

2. To generate customer action during "slow" times of the year.

3. To get tournament players into the casino where, it is hoped, they will spend some of their *non*-tournament time gambling at the tables. In this sense, a tournament functions as a "lure"—getting customers into the gaming establishment where it is hoped he or she will spend additional periods of time gambling.

4. To generate free local, national, and even international media coverage. Successful tournaments bring sponsoring casinos mega-bucks worth of positive publicity.

5. To stimulate gambling revenue through the play of non-tournament guests who cheer on their favorites... and do a little gambling of their own.

Who Wins Casino Gaming Tournaments?

Tournament sponsors are quick to claim that *anyone* can win their big-money events. In fact, they stress their tournaments are made-to-order for the "recreational player." Are they accurate? Can amateurs—weekend gamblers—come home with thousands of dollars in their pockets?

Well, yes... if the tournaments involve games of chance: games like craps, roulette, keno, slots, baccarat... tournaments where luck, *rather than skill*, determines the outcome. It is fair to say that anyone familiar with the basic rules of the game being played has a chance of winning.

Recreational gamblers also have a chance of winning tournaments involving games of skill... if the tournament is structured to limit the impact of skilled play (e.g., short playing sessions) and enhance the impact of "luck" on the outcome of the contest. Such is the case with almost all casino blackjack tournaments.

In this light, it is instructive to get a feel for the kinds of people who have already won tournaments. Many years ago, I did an analysis of players who had won International Gaming Promotions (IGP) blackjack tournaments over an eight-year period.

If you think that most blackjack winners came from states with casino gambling you'd be wrong. Of the first 47 champions only *one* lived in Nevada or New Jersey. Approximately 33 percent of the winners lived in California and 15 percent resided in the state of New York. The other 50-plus percent lived in residences scattered throughout the country.

What about the occupations of various winners? Were most of them professional gamblers or employed in gaming-related jobs? Hardly. Except for one champion who was a cardroom owner, the jobs held by winners read like a vocational dictionary. Here are some of the occupations of IGP blackjack champions during the period of my survey: Retired plasterer... truck salesman... retired grocer... chief investigator, DA's office, Napa, California... businessman... petroleum distributor... podiatrist... businessman... equipment distributor... Realtor... agricultural engineer... antique book dealer... insurance salesman... retired air force Lt. Col... CPA... candy store owner... engineer... retired carpenter... food inspector... garbage company co-owner... pizza parlor owner... West-

ern Auto Parts owner... oil well servicing contractor...
homemaker... manager... newspaperman... restaurant
owner... mortgage broker... attorney.

Are there any casino tournaments where the recreational
player is at a disadvantage and not favored to win? Yes.
The professional gambler has his or her best chance of
beating the amateur in major poker tournaments, particularly the big-money, multiple-day, freeze-outs that allow
the knowledgeable player sufficient opportunity to prevail over less-polished adversaries. Binion's World Series
of Poker is a classic example of this kind of tournament.

In summary, then, anyone has a chance to win a casino
tournament as long as:

1.   the contestant has a basic familiarity with the game
     being played; and

2.   the competition involves games of chance (e.g., craps,
     roulette, slots, keno, baccarat) or contests that are
     structured to limit the skill factor as a significant vari-
     able in play (e.g., tournament blackjack).

How Should You Choose A Tournament?

By now some of you might be chomping at the bit,
anxious to try your hand at tournament gaming. But
please—before you take off in search of gold and glory
ask yourself: "Which tournament is best for me?"

If you want to get the most for your tournament dollar,
it is vital that you shop around and select the tournament
that gives you the best chance of winning the greatest
amount of money for the least possible investment. To

accomplish this objective you'll need to ask—and answer—the following questions:

1. **What kind of tournaments are available?** If you don't live in a casino town, it isn't always easy to find out. The best sources for learning about upcoming tournaments are (a) national gaming magazines, (b) casino newsletters or announcements, and (c) the Internet. If you write to the casinos you would be interested in visiting, and request a schedule of their tournaments, they will be more than happy to keep you informed of coming events.

2. **Do the tournaments fit my playing schedule?** Dedicated tournament players plan their gaming trips around specific tournament dates. That way they don't have to incur extra travel costs to attend the tournament of their choice.

3. **What will the tournament cost me?** Tournaments aren't usually free (unless you are a premium player getting a free entry to encourage your visit to the host casino). You'll want to know the entry fee and, if relevant, the buy-in requirements for play. Contemporary tournaments hardly ever require buy-ins anymore, so in most cases the entry fee will be your only concern.

    It is crucial that you select a tournament with entry fee or buy-in costs that are appropriate to your normal level of play. Just as you should never make wagers larger than you can comfortably afford to lose, neither should you enter tournaments where your costs are too large for your bankroll to comfortably accommodate.

4. **Does the tournament allow for "re-entry" rounds?**
    When a person travels a long way to play in a tournament, the opportunity to get a "second chance" can be a determining factor in tournament selection.

5. **What is the prize structure?** Here you will want to know how much money or prizes can be won. What you are looking for are tournaments that (a) return the greatest proportion of the player's entry fee in awards; and (b) give the largest possible prizes for the smallest possible player investment.

    Also of importance to consider: Is the player allowed to keep all of his or her winnings at the tables? Do players receive prizes for winning preliminary sessions (before the championship round)? Do players get an entry fee reduction for early payment of fees (the so-called "early bird" rate)? Are there any gifts given to players for entering the tournament? Do players get a "break" on room and food rates in the hotel hosting the tournament? Are the top cash prizes guaranteed, or is the amount of the prize dependent on the number of participants who actually play in the tournament?

6. **How many opponents must be beaten to win the significant prize(s)?** The fewer people you must beat to win the money... the better!

In summary, what you are looking for is a tournament that offers you the best odds (fewest people to beat) to win the biggest possible prize(s) with the lowest out-of-pocket expenses. Such a situation arises most often when a casino is willing to lose money on the tournament in hopes of gaining significant media exposure or enlarging its premium customer base.

From an entertainment point of view, tournaments are great bargains. The thrill of the competition, the opportunity to make new friends, the hospitality of the host casino—all these factors make tournaments unforgettable experiences. Don't miss out on these tournament benefits. Make every attempt to attend the banquets, parties, and ceremonies given in your behalf. You won't regret it.

See you at the final table!

CHAPTER 21

Question #6:

"Do Casinos Cheat?"

The moment I spotted Marty, I knew something was amiss. What was he doing walking into an Atlantic City restaurant at 3 p.m., a time he faithfully reserved for his afternoon blackjack play.

"Hey, Marty, what's up?" I asked. "Why aren't you at the tables?"

Marty shrugged his shoulders. "No more blackjack for me," he said flatly.

"I heard you've been losing a bit lately," I confided sympathetically. "but that's no reason to throw in the towel. The cards will turn."

"Not when the game is crooked."

"Crooked?" I didn't try to hide my surprise. "Have you been playing in private games?"

"No." Marty had a disgusted look on his face. "I've been playing in casinos. Atlantic City. Vegas. And the games are crooked... a bunch of double dealers and bust-out mechanics."

"Are you sure?"

"Of course I'm sure," he snapped. "How else could I be a loser with the odds in my favor?"

In fact, there are many ways Marty could be a loser with the odds in his favor, not the least of which is improper play at the tables. And, considering Marty's tendency to "steam" when he lost a few hands, such a possibility wasn't exactly remote. It wouldn't be the first time a gambler blamed his losses on cheating dealers rather than on his own poor play.

What worried me about Marty's attitude was this: **A gambler's belief that he is being cheated can affect his play—his psychobiological edge—whether, in fact, he is being cheated or not.** In the case of Marty, his belief caused him to end his play altogether, an action he surely wouldn't have contemplated had he attributed his recent losses to improper play or a "run of bad cards."

In the case of other gamblers I have known, the fear of being cheated has affected their play by diverting their attention to the dealer rather than the game. And, of course, there is also the issue of enjoyment; If you think you're being cheated in the casino, the pleasure of gaming is going to be reduced. After all, whom do you know that relishes the idea of being swindled out of their bankroll? Which brings us to the pertinent question. What about cheating by the casinos?

Might a casino seek the ultimate house edge and *cheat* you out of your money? After all, with all that cut-throat competition for the gamblers' dollars, couldn't it be a temptation for some unscrupulous casino operators to fatten their profit margins by ordering a little hanky-panky at the tables?

Let me respond to the cheating issue in this way: Every gambler must recognize that casino personnel—owners, managers, dealers—are human beings. And being human they are fallible. They can be tempted and they can be dishonest. In other words, they can cheat. And they do. In fact, the Gaming Control Board, which oversees gambling operations in Nevada, has closed several casinos for cheating over the years.

But—and this is a very important "but"—cheating in contemporary Nevada and other major casino destinations is extremely rare. So rare, in fact, that the average player will probably never encounter any in a lifetime of casino visits. Winning gamblers, particularly those who win *big*, run a higher risk of being cheated, but they can avoid that risk by keeping their playing sessions short (60 minutes or less) and spreading their play among different casinos.

In reality, when it comes to cheating in major American and foreign casinos, there are many more incidents of players trying to cheat the house than vice versa.

Playing It Safe

Do not underestimate the psychological value of playing in an honest casino. When you don't have to worry about being cheated, you can play more effectively, concentrating on the game rather than on quick-handed dealers. One major reason people gamble in established, legal casinos in the first place is the peace of mind they have in knowing that things are on the up and up. Give yourself a fair shake—**never** play in unregulated (illegal) casinos where cheating is always a possibility. It just isn't a safe bet.

Your best defense against cheating is to limit your casino gambling *exclusively* to large, successful, legalized establishments in this country and abroad. The odds of encountering cheating at these casinos are extremely small. The owners have too much to lose (revocation or suspension of a casino license can mean losses in the millions), and—considering the way most players gamble—there is no need to cheat because, as a gaming authority friend of mine observed, the games in themselves are a "license to steal."

Another way to protect yourself against being cheated is to learn crooked moves and how to spot them. This is extremely difficult, what with the number of possible moves and the problems in detecting them. In the hands of a polished cheat, crooked moves are literally impossible to spot.

The hand is truly quicker than the eye, particularly untrained eyes like mine... or yours. Let's face it, if a skilled card mechanic wants to cheat you, he'll be able to. Your best defense is to gamble in a place where dealers *won't* want to.

There is a third way to protect yourself against cheats, but you'll have to lose for a while before you can use it. Here's how the method works: Each time you play, be alert for any *highly* unusual gambling results. If you find yourself losing *far* more than normal, or greatly in excess of what mathematical probability would predict, then you should quit at once and avoid playing in that establishment again.

Perhaps your losses weren't due to cheating—after all, mathematical probabilities do allow for highly unusual runs of cards and dice. Maybe you just ran into a mathematically rare event at the tables. There's really no way to tell (without actually *spotting* any crooked moves). But why take any chances? There are plenty of other places you can gamble; why stay at a casino where you consistently lose? If nothing else, maybe a change of playing locations will improve your psychological outlook and get you back on the winning track.

Here's a final way to defend yourself against cheating: Don't gamble too long in any one casino, particularly if you are in a rare period of *consistent* winning at a game the casino knows can be beaten. By gambling an hour or less in each casino and then moving on, you make it difficult for casino management to assess your winning potential or to do anything about it. If you employ this "hit and run" strategy, your chances of being cheated due to your being a winner should be close to zero.

CHAPTER 22

Question #7:

Can I Make A Living At Casino Gambling?

Casinos are not built from funds supplied
by winning gamblers.

Burt Friedman, CPA

After reading this book, some of you might be tempted
to quit your job, pack your bags, and head out to your
"friendly" casino for some fun, merriment, and steady
income.

Don't!

There are people—very few, I might add—who *can*
make a living from playing in the casino but, unless pos-
sessed of some very rare skills and personal qualities,
you won't be one of them.

Playing at positive-expectation games that can be beaten
with consistency, and having the skill to accomplish the
victory, are two different things. Don't kid yourself into
thinking you have the skills necessary when you don't.

Winning over the long run is extremely difficult even for those *with* the skills necessary, requiring the player to exercise a high level of patience, perseverance, talent, and self-control on a daily basis.

And the casino doesn't make it any easier. Take blackjack, as an example. Since the 1960s, when the publications of Edward Thorp made it clear that 21 could be beaten, the casinos have instituted a host of countermeasures designed to thwart the "professional" and make winning much more difficult, if not impossible. From one-deck blackjack with player-friendly rules to multideck blackjack with casino-friendly rules, the game has become almost unbeatable. Add to this (1) the casino's right to "shuffle-up" whenever they suspect a "professional" at work, (2) poor cut-card penetration, plus (3) the harassment of winning players, and you have a formula for gambling tragedy. One seasoned professional blackjack player put things into perspective with this telling observation:

> In the 1970s, playing blackjack put bread in my pocket and bread on the table. In the 1980s, playing blackjack put bread on my table. In the 1990s, playing blackjack took dough out of my pocket and left my table bare.

Things aren't easy for the casino poker player, either. In his book *Texas Hold'em Poker*, professional player Ken Warren tells why:

"Theoretically, poker is a zero-sum game. Your loss is another player's gain. The total amount of money put into the game remains the same, it just gets redistributed as the game goes on. If ten players with $100 each sit in a game it is possible for one player to eventually win all $1,000.

"But that's not possible when you play in a casino because of the 'rake.' The rake is a percentage of the pot that the casino takes out of each pot to compensate them for the cost of providing the dealers, chips, the poker table, and all the other overhead. If you play long enough in a raked game, the house will eventually have all the money. Now, instead of one player winning the $1,000, the house will win the money, $2, $3 or $4 at a time. The house will have all the money on the table in three or four hundred hands."

After that sobering commentary, Mr. Warren gives us further pause for concern when he concludes:

"The rake is taken out of the winner's pot. Remember that every time you enter a pot you're exposing yourself to the house rake, the jackpot drop, and the dealer's toke if you win the hand. You need to play pretty good poker to beat all that, and nine other players too."

My Recommendation

Winning in the casino is never easy. Winning steadily enough to achieve a successful gambling career is even more difficult, if not downright impossible.

Very few individuals have what it takes to maintain interest and profits over the long run. First, if you think you are one of these rare persons, prove you can consistently beat the *positive-expectation* game you are playing.

Second, keep in mind that evolving casino countermeasures will probably make your winning considerably more difficult in the future. Third, examine the hours you'll have to play and the money you'll have to risk in order to make a gambling "job" worthwhile. And fourth, ask yourself if you'll still enjoy gambling once the novelty wears off and you're *required* to do it year after year to make a living.

When you've given some thoughtful consideration to these four points, I suspect you'll decide against a casino gambling career. Good choice! I can tell you that after a similar examination, I rejected such a career choice *in a hurry*. To paraphrase the old saying: A casino is a great place to visit, but I wouldn't want to work there.

CHAPTER 23

Question #8:

What Is A "Compulsive" Gambler?

> To make a mistake is human. To learn from
> it is wisdom.
>
> *Anonymous*

Throughout this book I have provided you with tactics to make you a *tough* player, the kind of player casino managers fear the most.

But what if you can't—or won't—follow my recommendations? One possibility is you're stubborn and just want to do things *your* way. A more ominous possibility, however, is you've crossed over the line to compulsion.

What is a compulsive gambler? Players ask me this question more than any other, possibly because they know I'm a psychologist and figure I have a pat answer to their inquiry. In fact, a precise definition of compulsive gambling can be an elusive goal, difficult to achieve. It is much like trying to define "pornography".... and I am reminded of the judge who, when asked to define "smut," answered: "I can't tell you what it is, but I sure can recognize it when I see it."

Yet, the difficulty encountered in trying to define compulsive gambling is no excuse to ignore the problem or its impact on people's lives. In fact, **it is vital that each of us accurately and honestly assess our own gaming behavior—keeping alert for any telltale signs that might suggest an inability to control our play at the tables.**

Are *You* A Compulsive Gambler?

To help you assess your own gambling behavior, take a look at the following list of questions provided by Gamblers Anonymous. As you read through each item, ask yourself: *"Does this describe the way I am?"* Try to be as honest and objective as you can in answering each item.

1. Have you ever lost time from work due to gambling?

2. Has gambling ever made your home life unhappy?

3. Has gambling affected your reputation?

4. Have you ever felt remorse after gambling?

5. Have you ever gambled to get money with which to pay debts or otherwise solve financial difficulties?

6. Has gambling caused a decrease in your ambition or efficiency?

7. After losing, have you felt that you must return as soon as possible and win back your losses?

8. After a win, do you have a strong urge to return and win more?

9. Have you often gambled until your last dollar was gone?

10. Have you ever borrowed to finance your gambling?

11. Have you ever sold anything to finance gambling?

12. Have you been reluctant to use gambling money for normal expenditures?

13. Has gambling made you careless of the welfare of yourself and your family?

14. Have you ever gambled longer than you had planned?

15. Have you ever gambled to escape worry or trouble?

16. Have you ever committed or considered committing an illegal act to finance gambling?

17. Has gambling caused you to have difficulty in sleeping?

18. Do arguments, disappointments, or frustrations create within you an urge to gamble?

19. Have you ever had an urge to celebrate any good fortune by a few hours of gambling?

20. Have you ever considered self-destruction as a result of your gambling?

What Should You Do If You Think You Might Be A Compulsive Gambler?

Your course of action is clear. GET PROFESSIONAL HELP. And stop gambling altogether. I know that sounds harsh. It's meant to. If you're a compulsive gambler, you have a powerful addiction. It can destroy you emotionally as well as financially.

Please recall my earlier observation: It is vital that each of you accurately and honestly assess your own behavior—determine for yourself whether you can control your play at the casino. If, after reading this book, you decide you cannot control your gambling... then you will be well-advised to eliminate it from your life.

Controlled gambling can be fun and challenging. Gambling out of control is a bet you can't win. It's a gamble not worth taking.

TOGA!

For the past fifteen years, I've been using psycho-biological principles to train commercial airline pilots. During this time, I learned that some airlines have an interesting way to handle emergencies that occur during the final stage of descent into an airport. If any member of the cockpit crew deems that a safe landing is in jeopardy, he or she calls out "TOGA" (TOGoAround), and the landing attempt is immediately aborted. No questions. No discussion. Thrust is applied to the engines and the plane "goes around" for another try when safety concerns have been resolved.

I've always thought that gamblers could make good use of the aviator's "TOGA" idea. How many times have you been at the tables or slots when you sense things are going seriously wrong? Maybe the dice or cards turn suddenly cold... or possibly you sense yourself losing control as you begin chasing your losses or borrowing money not allotted for gambling so you can keep in action.

What should you do? Yell, "TOGA!" and get the hell out of there! Pull up! Pull up! Firewall the engines and take off! Get away from the casino before you crash and burn. Get some altitude and give yourself a chance to assess your "gamble-worthiness." Make sure you are back in control and safe before you decide to put down in the casino again.

And here's one final thing you'll want to know. When TOGA is declared and the crew "goes around," they don't always end up at the airport where they abort the landing. Sometimes they're required to fly to an "alternate" (aviator jargon for another airport) to find the conditions necessary for a safe arrival at the gate.

How about you? If you can't land safely at a casino destination, maybe it's time you considered an alternate landing site... someplace where you won't be putting yourself and your loved ones at risk. *Maybe it's time that you quit gambling altogether.*

If you love gambling as much as I do, a decision to quit gambling permanently will be one of the most difficult decisions you'll ever make. Yet, it is a decision that must be made if you are to ensure your financial survival and personal self-esteem in the years ahead.

TOGA! Aviators use it to get us safely from point A to point B. You use it to get yourself safely from the casiono to your home.
Bon Voyage!

Other Great Gambling Titles
From Gollehon Books

Video Poker Mania (Crevelt)

Slot Machine Mania (Crevelt)

Casino Games (Gollehon)

Casino Games II (Gollehon)

Casino Gambling Behind The Tables (Alcamo)

Las Vegas Behind The Tables (Vinson)

Las Vegas Behind The Tables, Part 2 (Vinson)

Conquering Casino Craps (Gollehon)

The Book Casino Managers Fear The Most (Karlins)

A Gambler's Little Instruction Book (Gollehon)

Beat The Track (Kulleck)

Casino Comics (Lewis)

Deadly Deception (Engelhard)

Casino Gambling For Boneheads (Gollehon)

Other Books Authored
Or Co-Authored
By Marvin Karlins

Novels:

Gomorrah (Doubleday)

The New Atoms Bombshell (Ballantine)

The Last Man Is Out (Prentice-Hall)

The Grey Avengers (Gollehon)

Trade Non-Fiction:

Biofeedback (Lippincott)

Requiem For Democracy?
(Holt, Rinehart & Winston)

The Other Way To Better Grades (Fawcett)

Psyching Out Vegas (Lyle Stuart)

Education For Freedom (John Wiley)